frozen

couple's path from "life on hold"
to adoption

MIKE BUTCHER

Published by
British Association for Adoption & Fostering
(BAAF)
Saffron House
6–10 Kirby Street
London EC1N 8TS
www.baaf.org.uk

Charity registration 275689 (England & Wales)
and SC039337 (Scotland)

British Library Cataloguing in Publication Data
A catalogue record for this book is available from
the British Library

ISBN 978 1 905664 92 4

Project management by Shaila Shah, Director of Publications, BAAF
Cover design by Helen Joubert
Designed by Andrew Haig & Associates
Typeset by Fravashi Aga
Printed in Great Britain by T J International
Trade distribution by Turnaround Publisher Services, Unit 3,
Olympia Trading Estate, Coburg Road, London N22 6TZ

BAAF is the leading UK-wide membership organisation for all
child care issues.

is FSC certified.
nternational network
rld's forests.

FSC

Mixed Sources
Product group from well-managed
forests and other controlled sources

Cert no. SGS-COC-2482
www.fsc.org
© 1996 Forest Stewardship Council

Contents

Acknowledgements

Thanks to my amazing wife, Lesley, for her extensive input to this book, her uncanny knack for detail, and for letting me write all these things about her; to Ellen for being there and to Gwen for knowing what to do; to Raul Margara, Stuart Lavery and the staff of Queen Charlotte's Hospital, without whom this book would have had a very different ending; to Hedi, for saving me from some of my worst jokes; to all our family and friends whose support kept us sane through everything; and a very special thanks to Maureen, Ann, Monica, Lynda and Bob – you know what you did and we owe you all so much.

Note

Everyone mentioned in this book has played some part in trying to help Lesley and I build a family and for that we are very grateful. Some of the names of these people and the hospitals we have attended have been changed or withheld out of respect for their privacy or indeed our own. The notable exceptions to this are our family and friends, the consultants at Queen Charlotte's Hospital and our local council's social workers – all of whom have been asked and have agreed to be named, and whose special contributions to our story we felt compelled to recognise personally.

About the author

Mike Butcher's addiction to writing began when he supplemented his student grant producing articles for IPC Magazines' *2000AD* comic. He went on to spend eight years working in the comic book industry, writing and editing magazines and comics that featured characters from TV shows such as *Rainbow*, *Postman Pat* and *Red Dwarf*, among many others. His previous books include Hamlyn's *A to Z of Judge Dredd*, a guide to the 1996 Olympics, published by Ladybird, and several children's Christmas annuals.

For Lesley
and our special little boy

The Our Story series
This book is part of BAAF's Our Story series, which explores adoption and fostering experiences as told by adoptive parents and foster carers.

Also available in the series:

The series editor
Hedi Argent is an independent family placement consultant, trainer and freelance writer. She is the author of *Find me a Family* (Souvenir Press, 1984), *Whatever Happened to Adam?* (BAAF, 1998), *Related by Adoption* (BAAF, 2004), *One of the Family* (BAAF, 2005), *Ten Top Tips for Placing Children in Families* (BAAF, 2006), *Josh and Jaz have Three Mums* (BAAF, 2007), *Ten Top Tips for Placing Siblings* (BAAF, 2008), and *Ten Top Tips for Supporting Kinship Placements* (BAAF, 2009). She is the co-author of *Taking Extra Care* (BAAF, 1997, with Ailee Kerrane) and *Dealing with Disruption* (BAAF, 2006, with Jeffrey Coleman), and the editor of *Keeping the Doors Open* (BAAF, 1988), *See You Soon* (BAAF, 1995), *Staying Connected* (BAAF, 2002), and *Models of Adoption Support* (BAAF, 2003). She has also written five illustrated booklets in the children's series published by BAAF: *What Happens in Court?* (2003, with Mary Lane), *What is Contact?* (2004), *What is a Disability?* (2004), *Life Story Work* (2005, with Shaila Shah) and *What is Kinship Care?* (2007).

Email

From: **Lesley Butcher**
To: **Claire Cheshire**
Date: **17 May 2001**

Mike is getting really stressed with this course of IVF. I've never seen him like this before. I think he is just terrified that it could go wrong again. People don't think of how much it hurts the men, they only think of the women.

I am going into hospital tomorrow for my egg collection. We have had a bit of a setback though. Do you remember me telling you about ovarian hyper-stimulation? Basically, if I produce too many follicles when they inject me to release the eggs it could make me really ill. Well, sod's law, when I went for a scan last night hoping for maybe 10 follicles, I had about 30 on one ovary.

It's definitively too dangerous to go for an implant straight after egg collection. So any eggs they collect tomorrow will be fertilised and then the embryos will be frozen for me to use as and when I like. All I need to do is pop down to Iceland!

The whole thing has been really painful. If you can imagine an ovary being the size of a lemon, then mine are currently the size of small melons and are crushing every organ of my body. I have been awake since three o'clock this morning, tossing and turning, trying to get comfortable. Never mind, it will all be over soon.

1

Frozen

It is around 23 degrees Celsius outside today. That's a scorcher for this time of year. Sure, we had rain earlier and a rash of lightning bolts pierced the sky, but all that was just clearing the air for the bright sunshine that followed. I think I even felt warm at some point. But I don't right now. In fact I'm frozen. Frozen by fear. Chilled with thoughts I find hard to comprehend. And trapped in a bubble of time that seems to have swallowed me whole and drawn all the heat from my body. I shouldn't be feeling this way, but I do. Things have taken a pretty weird turn lately, but it's not that. Weird I can handle. There's something else and it scares me half to death.

Friday 18 May 2001

The procedure went well this morning. The egg collection from Lesley's ovaries yielded no less than 20 eggs ripe for impregnation. A stunning success by anyone's standards. Of course, getting here has been tough, requiring a large pile of fertility drugs, dozens of injections, plenty of hard cash, countless scans and, yes, we have had some anxious moments.

People often talk about the stresses and strains of "in-vitro fertilisation treatment", or IVF for short, and my wife's and my experiences have been right up there with the worst of them – so far. It's an unnatural situation to be in, as a whole load of things that really should be happening quite naturally have become part of a carefully calculated set of scientific protocols.

Even with the highly professional staff of a top-notch private fertility clinic guiding us through this process with great care and consideration, there are aspects of what we have to do that seem designed to freak out the most well adjusted participant. Personally, I don't think I will ever get used to the idea of giving Lesley those daily injections in the soft tissue just under her skin. It does my head in and I've never felt stress like it.

It's almost enough to get me thinking about the alternatives to all this medical intervention – we already have a cat, so that just leaves (a) hand-carving a wooden boy Pinnochio-style and hoping that a Blue Fairy comes by one day, (b) plotting some kind of diabolical child abduction scheme or (c) adoption, but this last option in particular sounds like a whole new world of stress we are not about to contemplate right now.

In any case, we're not the kind of people to fold under a little bit of pressure. We're strong, we're sure we can get through anything and we know the end result will be worth it, whatever it takes. After all, how bad can it get? We are in good hands at a plush private hospital just a few miles from home, and these guys have carried out all this treatment thousands of times before. Success or failure, we know we can cope.

Through bitter experience, if nothing else.

We've had a taste of failure already, because we've made it this far once before. During our first attempt at full IVF there were just as many injections – possibly more. So many "ampules", or doses of the stuff, that it became quite tricky to talk about the drugs we were using in public without sounding like we were the UK's connection for a South American cocaine cartel.

The drug in question is Puragon, the purest form of fertility drug money can buy, so I'm told. All natural, and the most effective thing on the market, it says on the packet. Carbon neutral, I dare say, and kind to fluffy animals too. None of your artificial fertility drug substitutes for us, and boy, do we have the bills to prove it.

The thing is, during this first attempt, Puragon just wouldn't work. A standard dose of one ampule injected daily ought to be enough to kick those ovaries into action. Nothing. A couple of weeks in and our specialist upped the dose to two, then three. Still nothing. Four. Still nothing. Five weeks in, we were at six ampules per injection and I was expecting the cartel to put the squeeze on me any day soon.

In fact, because our drug bills were escalating so high during that attempt, the team at the hospital actually took pity on us and gave us some spare Puragon for free that had been returned by another patient.

Despite all our heart-rending effort and this unexpected generosity, we were about to give up when bingo, a reaction at last. The agony, it seemed, was finally over. A number of follicles had grown and could be seen on a scan of one of Lesley's ovaries. No less than seven "oocytes" were successfully collected from them a couple of days later. It was a great result after almost six weeks of despair.

An oocyte, by the way, is a posh medical term for a human egg, and if nothing else it provides a very good way of getting rid of a handful of Os in *Scrabble*.

What follows the collection of these infinitely precious but terrifyingly vulnerable pin-prick sized parcels of life is a kind of microbiological version of *Big Brother*, with eviction nights coming thick and fast until you have a couple of finalists, but more often than not, no winner.

Some oocytes are deemed to be of too poor a quality to be useful and it's basically *game over* for them. Of the remaining eggs, some fertilise and become embryos while others don't, but no one can really explain why. Then some of the hardiest embryos' cells grow and multiply, while their next-door neighbours simply sit there sulking and refuse to do the same – before making their exit to jeers and cheers, without even a comforting word from Davina McCall.

When examined up close like this, all the fun and games around egg retrieval, incubation and fertilisation give you a harsh and very direct exposure to the true lottery of life. You start to wonder how any of us ever gets born at all without this kind of help and you have to marvel at the astonishing amount of luck it has taken to produce the six billion or so people alive in the world today.

My immediate job following the egg collection during that first full IVF cycle was to carry a special incubator strong box with those hard earned eggs from the local hospital to a clinic in Harley Street, home of so many of London's most exclusive (and expensive) private medical consultants. The area is famous for treating the bunions or whatever of the great and the good, and coming to the aid of all those reality TV "celebrities" in search of vital plastic surgery. I wasn't sure they would even let me in, but I jumped into my car to start my journey anyway.

Before I set off, I was supposed to plug the incubator box into the car's cigarette lighter socket to provide power to help keep the contents safe and warm. Unfortunately, I couldn't make the plug attachment fit the socket. Every time I tried, the plug simply fell out of the box. Alarmed, I rushed back inside to seek advice, but the doctor in charge of the fertility unit at the hospital told me not to worry about it. The incubator box's battery power is supposed to last three to four hours on its own, so I put my foot down and drove.

Freshly harvested eggs need around three hours of incubation at body temperature anyway before the fun really starts and you need to get cracking with the fertilisation process, so time was on my side. Didn't feel like it though, as I swept down the M40 into London.

Talk about pressure.

When I arrived at the embryology clinic, I had to provide a fresh sperm sample to be matched with the eggs. And if you have ever wondered whether this is as awkward and embarrassing as you might imagine, you should see the grotty rooms they put you in at one of these places on Harley Street with a tatty old copy of *Razzle* and a small plastic container with a screw top.

But human dignity has very little to do with the IVF process and I knew that a man's gotta do what a man's gotta do. The worst part was carrying the still-warm specimen container around to the embryologists' door in the clinic's basement. Then knocking rather sheepishly and handing over the container. I defy anyone to do this with a degree of chirpy self-assurance. I certainly didn't.

Armed with all the necessary ingredients, the embryology team then busied themselves with their centrifuge machines, Petri dishes, kitchen blenders, super-powerful microscopes and whatever else they needed to get on with fertilising our seven eggs.

We had been advised that the "intra-cytoplasmic sperm injection" or ICSI procedure, an even more specialised variant on standard IVF, would be most suitable in our case. ICSI is now commonly recommended to couples seeking IVF treatment, as it takes away many of the issues with the randomness or absence of sperm motility, and a lot of that messy jiggling of test tubes.

It's more expensive though, a fact of life Lesley and I are

becoming quite accustomed to in the world of private fertility treatment.

I have learned a few more things about ICSI too. First off, it would seem that it was invented by accident – a pure fluke! No one ever imagined you could inject a single sperm into a single egg with any chance at all that it would survive the assault. Obviously, it would be much too fragile. Stands to reason, doesn't it? But someone did it anyway, without even meaning to (although quite how that happened is anyone's guess). And would you believe it, the egg not only survived, it flourished and developed into a viable embryo.

Taking advantage of this astonishing breakthrough, our seven eggs and seven sperm combined to become four viable embryos overnight, with three unlucky pairs missing out on their chance for life at this earliest possible stage.

One of the survivors completely failed to divide into two or more cells, while another managed this minor feat, but lagged miserably behind in its development and generally sat there feeling sorry for itself. Unfortunately there are no special classes to help you catch up at Embryo School, so that was two down, two to go. The remaining embryos were allowed to multiply to six or eight cells in their specially prepared dishes over the next couple of days, until both of them were ready to be returned to Lesley.

You can watch television shows or read books about IVF and everything that comes with it, but when you are in the middle of it all, things go by in something of a blur until you make an effort to stop and really think about what is actually happening. Human eggs, sperm, even embryos – these things are small. Pinhead small. Or in the case of that cheeky little sperm fellow, much much smaller. You can't see any of them with the naked eye and yet there they are living outside of the human body, something they are definitely not designed to do.

Not only that, but the whole point of all this is that one

of these tiny specks might just grow into a real live child one day, assuming that it can successfully check into a cosy womb for about nine months at some point and negotiate the whole birthing process without mishap.

Our two battle-hardened embryos were duly implanted inside Lesley's womb a few days later, during a procedure as undignified as has become the norm for us these days and we waited to see if they'd managed to hang onto something in there to bed themselves in.

Unfortunately, the chances of a single IVF cycle working are well south of 20 per cent and we soon found out that we weren't the lucky one in five that time.

So here we are again. This time I have a box full of 20 eggs, a bumper crop, and getting to this stage has taken a fraction of the time. Less than two weeks in fact – although this acceleration has only been achieved by using the maximum dose of six ampules of our good friend Puragon each day. By starting out at the higher dose, our IVF consultant has succeeded in provoking the desired response from Lesley's ovaries on a much tighter schedule than last time. If anything, the number of follicles that have grown this time around seems a little excessive, but at least we haven't had to endure an agonising six-week wait for them to arrive.

And we have 20 eggs! That's got to be good, right? So why do I feel such trepidation? Not just now, but even before we started out on this second IVF attempt. For some strange reason I cannot begin to understand, I have had a bad feeling about all this for a while. And the nurses here aren't really reassuring me now, with looks of concern betraying the smiles they give me as they hand over the precious cargo.

The last thing Julia, the lead practice nurse at the hospital, says to me is 'Freeze all'. This is confirming a course of action that has been decided on over the past couple of days, but I haven't really kept up with the whys and wherefores. There have been far too many other things for me to worry about and I'm not entirely sure what she means by this. But time's a wasting, so I point the car towards Harley Street and put my foot down.

The cigarette lighter socket's not working again, so I'd better hurry. Mustn't let the eggs get cold, what kind of father would I be if I allowed that to happen?

Same routine at the embryology clinic, except the first thing they say to me on presentation of the still-warm specimen container when I knock at the embryologist's door is 'Freeze all?' I confirm the instruction and they return to their swirling, separating and injecting without another word.

Twenty eggs. That's got to be good, right?

Now I have a chance to think about things, I am more than a little vexed as all the bad feelings I have had about this treatment cycle for the past couple of weeks or so are beginning to resurface with a vengeance. And little voices are whispering into my ear, telling me that I have completely lost control of this situation.

I try to recall what we have already discussed with our consultant, but no one is telling me anything and my questions are piling up. Leaving the clinic in London, I'm none the wiser and head back to the hospital to see how Lesley is feeling as she recovers from the egg retrieval.

When I arrive she is groggy, but fine. Heavily sedated rather than unconscious during the procedure, Lesley had only one really cogent moment while it was all happening. I'm told that immediately following the egg collection, she sat bolt upright and asked how many they'd got. On hearing about the 20 eggs she lay back down and drifted off to sleep with a big smile on her face.

Not that Lesley remembers any of this now, but the fertility team have run through the situation with her again and I realise I was a fool to be worried earlier. The decision to freeze all is merely a precaution on these occasions and it is all about avoiding some of the unpleasant side effects of IVF treatment that arise in very rare cases. It means that any viable embryos that grow within the next couple of days will be deep frozen at the clinic and stored for later use. Everyone agrees that continuing with the treatment cycle at this stage would put Lesley at much greater risk.

To be honest, I am so stressed and yet somehow relieved that I still don't really take it all in. What I do hear is that this rich harvest has again come from just one of Lesley's ovaries, where no fewer than 50 follicles have grown. It is quite possible that a similar number may have developed on the other, apparently less accessible side, but we will never know. Best guess is that there may have been up to 70 eggs in all to choose from.

So now, despite Lesley's obvious delight at the time, I'm starting to wonder why we only retrieved *20 eggs*, as I'm pretty sure the incubator box was big enough to carry 50, 70 or even more. Before I get too greedy though, it may be time to look for some perspective here.

On a normal reproductive cycle, unaided by the wonders of Puragon, no woman would produce 70 eggs. Nor would their ovaries even consider yielding up 20, or even the seven of our previous attempt. No, there would be one. No more, no less, except on those relatively rare occasions when two might herald the potential arrival of non-identical twins. So 70 is a lot, around six years worth all in one go, in fact.

Who would have thought you could push the human body so hard and provoke such an extreme result as that?

And somewhere deep within my brain I start to hear those little voices again. Except this time, they come from a mob of middle European villagers, all carrying brightly lit torches while scampering up to the castle to burn it down and put a stop to all this Frankenstein science.

The embryologists at the clinic will call us on Monday

to let us know how many of the eggs have managed to vault the fertilisation hurdle. Before we even hear this all-important news, our lucky embryos will be packed into neat little tubes, or "straws", and find themselves entombed in liquid nitrogen at minus 196 degrees Celsius for up to five years long-term storage.

Tough break for them I reckon, but embryos can survive being frozen. I find that pretty amazing. Heads and brains can too, so they say, although to the best of my knowledge no one has yet worked out how to revive the likes of Walt Disney or any of his decapitated "cryo-pals" from their death-like slumber. By contrast, embryos are being woken up all the time, sometimes after many months or even years of being kept on ice in a state of cryopreservation.

The important thing is to freeze them correctly in the first place, of course. First you pop them into a series of solutions to draw out some of the water. This helps prevent the formation of ice crystals that could damage the embryo. Then you add what is known as a "cryoprotectant" to protect the embryos during freezing. The whole process takes about three hours, as the temperature is slowly decreased to minus 36 degrees Celsius before that final plunge into the liquid nitrogen.

In normal life, I realise that nothing like this is ever going to happen to you unless (a) you are part of a failed expedition trying to walk to the North Pole in your pyjamas, (b) you are stuck up a mountain in a particularly ferocious blizzard on the rescue team's day off, or (c) you find yourself in a cheap 1970s horror movie – you know the sort of film, something with Peter Cushing and Christopher Lee, clearly made while they were waiting for better offers, and an arbitrary cameo from Telly Savalas as a Cossack with a grudge.

We arrive home and happily there's no sign of any Cossacks, so Lesley gets herself off to bed for some much needed rest. For now, all we can do is wait for news on the embryos and, as it happens, eat. The fact is, Lesley is starving when we get home. The egg retrieval procedure, like most operations requiring anaesthesia of any kind, meant she had to pass on breakfast this morning and, apart from a cup of tea at the hospital, she has gone without any kind of nourishment since.

Somehow we have completely failed to foresee this situation and there is no food in the house, so we decide on a Chinese takeaway. We make the call and I nip out to fetch some noodles, chicken and a nice big silver dish of rice.

We eat, and it's a relief. Just about the only normal thing we have done today. I am actually starting to feel quite good again, when Lesley turns a funny colour and announces that she is going to be sick.

Now, I would never make a claim to having any kind of athletic prowess, but in certain situations I can react at a speed that belies my size. I have a bowl beside the bed within nanoseconds and I am eager to assist my poorly wife through a queasy moment following her earlier anaesthesia.

I am not expecting projectile vomiting.

The first wave sails past my ear and barely digested chicken hits the bedroom cabinet. The second wave covers my arm and there are noodles and rice everywhere. I look in the bowl. Nice try, but nothing. Lesley is mortified, she hates nothing more than throwing up, so I need to remain a picture of calm. It's only sick, I remind myself. Pretty spectacular sick I grant you, but this is all much worse for her than it is for me.

The nightmare continues as my wife proceeds to bring up all the food she has just eaten and I am pleased to see that the bowl has finally come into its own. The clean up is all the easier for it, but understandably Lesley is in pieces and she feels terrible. Ridiculously I ask her if she wants anything else to eat, but she prefers to get some sleep.

I wish there was more I could do, but the doctors have advised us – plenty of fluid, plenty of rest and Lesley will feel a lot better in a couple of days. Scant consolation when you've just said goodbye to your only decent meal in 24 hours and you feel like you've lost a fight with an angry rhinoceros. Oh, and they've taken almost a couple of dozen eggs out of one of your ovaries, had a go at fertilising them and are about to throw the survivors into the deep freeze. It's not been an average day in the Butcher household, but at least Lesley manages to get her head down.

So it's all quiet again now and I can't help thinking about that dimly recalled 1970s horror movie where a monster is entombed in ice for many years, and once released – big surprise – he goes berserk, seeking vengeance on everyone who put him there in the first place. I'm pretty sure that embryos never indulge in that kind of behaviour, but I really have no experience in this area. I am only marginally reassured by the fact that the monster in the film was already a crazed lunatic before being frozen and that this simply wouldn't happen with a normal person.

That's because a normal person would be dead. You could thaw him out, but he'd still be dead.

So how is an embryo supposed to survive that kind of treatment, I want to know? And as the evening wears on, what I am really wondering is how can my (potential) child be tough enough to live through something I couldn't possibly survive myself?

2

The lost weekend

What do you do when nine months before you have any chance of even being born, someone puts your life on hold? Do you feel the cold like I do? You should, it's minus 196 degrees Celsius out there, for goodness sake. And what if you're stuck in the middle of hundreds of other screaming embryos; wondering why you're in the freezer instead of snuggling up nice and warm inside your mother-to-be's womb? How do you survive? The principle of "survival of the fittest" is all very well, but when you're the size of a pinhead and encased in hermetically sealed ice, it's pretty hard to flex your muscles. If you had any to start with, that is. And these little guys don't – I know that much. Sorry Bob, Jim, Jane, Danny, Carol and the rest of you, you're all out of luck in the muscles department. And you're not breaking free of that ice any time soon.

Monday 21 May 2001
A weekend of troubled sleep later and here I am still

thinking dark thoughts, coldly contemplating the fate of my child.

Not the usual stuff: How will I cope when they get measles or chicken pox? Have they done their homework this week? Will they get into university? How can I keep them away from drugs / drink / fags / unsavoury elements of the opposite or even the same sex (delete as applicable)? How can I stop them crashing their car, beating their spouse, skinning the neighbour's hamster, or drowning in a ditch?

None of the above.

Nothing so trivial in fact. Instead I am trying to work out what chance he or she has of actually being born. And if that should ever happen, when might it be?

I was born 10 days later than expected. Nothing particularly unusual in that, 10 days is nothing. But I was born with a tooth! Odds against that are around 200,000-1, but Lesley says I'm one in a million, so no big deal. Our child could effectively be born a month late, several months late, or even several years late – as long as he or she can be successfully thawed out and then fully gestated. If this tooth thing runs in the family, the baby might come equipped with a full set of sharpened molars and will probably bite the midwife's arm clean off during the delivery.

It may have already become apparent, but I was also born with an overactive imagination, and I quickly realise that this is neither the time nor the place for it. I really am "weirded out" enough by the whole frozen embryo situation without painting ever more lurid images for myself about the months and years to come. Besides, Lesley is still feeling very unwell this morning and she needs me to be a bit more balanced and strong for her right now.

In fact, Lesley hasn't been her usual self all weekend and has spent most of the time either sleeping, or complaining about the swollen ovaries that have made it so uncomfortable for her to sleep. In between she has been trying, mostly unsuccessfully, to swallow small sips of water from the glass at her bedside.

She hasn't eaten anything since Friday's Chinese food eruption and to say that I am now very worried about her would be an understatement of epic proportions.

I talked to the lead practice nurse at the hospital on Saturday and she confirmed that Lesley must be suffering from a mild case of "ovarian hyper-stimulation syndrome", often referred to as OHSS on account of its unfeasibly long name and the desperate need to introduce another confusing acronym into our otherwise drab lives. OHSS, she explained, is one of the risks associated with stimulation of the ovaries: 'a rare condition that occurs when too many follicles grow and cause abdominal distension, discomfort, and nausea'.

Yep, that's three ticks for Lesley there, then. Lucky girl, she has no idea how *rare* she is.

In fact, OHSS is not really that rare at all and minor symptoms associated with the condition regularly show up during IVF treatment cycles. Generally, its effects are so moderate, it is hardly noticeable at all. Most women who suffer from it don't even realise they have experienced it and, on the whole, doctors don't recognise it, possibly because it is one of those afflictions none of them entirely understands.

The key phrase to look out for here is "too many follicles", and the threshold that usually triggers the warning buzzer is 20. Lesley's unwitting world record attempt of anything up to or perhaps even more than 70 follicles has probably tripped a couple of long-forgotten air raid sirens and the anti-tamper alert on our fertility consultant's shiny new sports car.

But it's OK, the doctors have recognised the condition in Lesley and they know how to tackle OHSS. I remember their advice. *Plenty of fluid, plenty of rest and Lesley will feel a lot better in a couple of days.* Nothing to worry about then, perhaps I should go to work today and leave Lesley to rest?

And I do. *What a complete and utter...*

Lesley's in bed, feeling worse than she has ever done in her whole life. She is feeling sick all the time, her whole body is hurting and she is stressed out because she's waiting for news of our embryos. By now, she's just about hungry enough to munch her way through the whole starting line-up of the 3.40 at Ascot, but is unable to keep even a few sips of water down. Yet I go to work because she assures me she's all right and will call me right away if she needs me. And, if I'm honest, because I need something to distract me from all the freaky stuff I've been brooding over for the past three days, before I go a bit mad.

Of course, when I get to work, all I can actually think about is Lesley and all the freaky stuff I've been brooding over for the past three days. I keep phoning her and waking her up. And after struggling to reach the phone as quickly as she can each time I call, because she thinks it's the clinic with news of our embryos, Lesley doesn't even sound pleased to hear from me. But I know she is.

'Have you been able to drink some water?' I ask her, and she says she's been trying.

With a glass of water in one hand and a bowl in the other, Lesley has been practising a new magic trick, which Tommy Cooper might have called "glass, water... water, bowl". This is not good. I have been told that the most important thing when you are suffering from mild OHSS is to stay hydrated. *Plenty of fluid.* So, how do you do that if you can't even drink water with any measurable degree of success?

I need some more advice, so I call one of the nurses at the private hospital's fertility unit. Again. This is getting a bit monotonous, but some reassurance would be good right now.

I should make it clear that they are a great bunch at the

hospital and we have got to know them well since our first appointment a couple of years ago. We were referred to their private fertility unit when the doctors at our local National Health hospital finally waved the white flag and said there was nothing more they could do for us.

Before that, between 1994 and 1999, we had trekked back and forth regularly to see one of the specialists at the maternity wing of the same NHS hospital. Lesley was diagnosed pretty early on with something called "polycystic ovarian syndrome", or PCOS for those of us keen to add yet another acronym to our growing collection. It is a common enough condition, which affects almost one in 20 women and is at the root of many a fertility problem.

PCOS has been well known since the 1930s, but the best minds in the field of gynaecology have never quite managed to pin down exactly what causes it. There are many symptoms, including irregular or heavy periods, but it also tends to mess with a woman's natural ability to produce eggs.

So before we ever pitched up at our cosy little private hospital, Lesley had popped countless pills prescribed by one doctor or another to deal with the problem. The pills were usually some variant of clomiphene, which turned out to be very good for regulating her periods, but pretty much useless when it came to anything else.

They even tried carrying out a laparoscopy – a delicate and less than pleasant procedure that involves checking out what's going on with your ovaries and, if the conditions are right, taking the opportunity to cauterise them while they are in there. As ghastly as it sounds, this can actually be a good thing and often sets things right. No such luck for Lesley though – the conditions were obviously not right as they didn't even complete the procedure. And that concluded the fertility treatment available to us under the postcode lottery operated by the NHS, as our local health authority would not even cover a single IVF treatment cycle.

Packed off to the private sector, we found a very different world at the little hospital. At last we were somewhere they had time for you, even if you did have to pay fairly handsomely for the privilege. Overall, it was like a breath of fresh air and the personal care and attention from the staff there took a lot of the stress and worry out of a daunting situation.

This afternoon, however, I am wondering where the limits to their good nature and practised patience lie. I know the team at the fertility unit care about Lesley, but when I voice my concerns for the third time in as many days, I can't shake the feeling that I'm becoming a bit of an irritant. They are very nice about it of course, but our treatment was last week and they have other patients to deal with today. They assure me that this sort of reaction is not so unusual following an IVF cycle, especially one that has come to an end like ours has done. Lesley needs to keep trying with her small sips of water and she will start feeling better soon.

I trust them, I really do, and I know that things will be OK, but I feel so helpless. I wish there was something more someone could do to help Lesley right now, because I've never seen her this unwell and it scares me.

Then I get a call from home and, for a moment, my whole world spins. Lesley sounds upset, my blood pressure spikes and my heart is pounding as I try to understand what might be wrong and listen to what she's telling me.

'It's about the embryos...no, I feel fine...the embryologist from the clinic just called with some news...'

And suddenly I remember just how many weird emotions we are both trying to juggle today. For a moment there I'd almost forgotten to obsess about the embryos. I should be worrying about how many of them have actually survived from our bountiful crop of 20 eggs. In particular, I ought to be stressing about their terrifying encounter with the liquid nitrogen. The poor little devils have nothing to look forward to except the inside of a pencil-sized ice stick for the foreseeable future.

The desperate plight of our embryos puts our fully-grown problems in some kind of perspective, so now I am keen to find out how many we have. Lesley quietly tells me that we have six embryos, all now packed carefully into their plastic tubes and wrapped up nice and cold in the clinic's best freezer. Apparently the embryologist sounded delighted with the news when he told her. Lesley was less enthusiastic. In fact her reaction five minutes ago was identical to mine now.

Six? Is that all, after everything we've been through? We had 20 on Friday, and all they've managed to get out of that bumper haul is a measly six?

These are not our exact words of course, but the thought is there and what we feel right now is disappointment.

'Well, that's great news, isn't it?' I offer and try to sound convincing.

Lesley agrees, doing no better at hiding the slight falter in her voice. We talk for a while, trying to make sense of things, and I grudgingly admit to myself that six isn't all that bad.

In fact, in the context of any normal IVF treatment cycle, it would be very good. It's just that this has been anything but a normal IVF cycle, and our hopes have been raised and dashed in not quite equal measures in the course of the last 72 hours or so. In the circumstances, we could do without "Mr Jolly the comedy embryologist" being so gleefully upbeat about the situation. He even offered to keep an eye on the embryos for us and promised Lesley that he would make sure they behave themselves in the freezer, before he finally hung up the phone and returned to whatever microbiological treat awaited him in the nearest Petri dish.

I guess we'll find out in a while if Mr Jolly is as good an

embryologist as he is a stand-up comedian. We sincerely hope a whole lot better.

I get home from work, and it's not late – though I can't help but feel that I've left Lesley for too long today. She still hasn't managed to keep any food or liquid down, the stomach pains are worse than ever and she is short of breath. I have never seen Lesley like this and I really don't like it. My sense of foreboding about this whole IVF cycle is growing by the minute and I still have no idea what to do about it. So I call the hospital again and tell them how worried I am. Being a stoic kind of a fellow, I try not to sound too desperate, but that is exactly how I am feeling.

'Perhaps Lesley has picked up a stomach bug,' they suggest. 'It happens sometimes.'

'Bollocks,' I reply.

Except it comes out as, 'do you really think so?'

At the height of your own panic, it is hard to take on the medical establishment and explain to them why you are right and they are wrong. I wish there were some way I could convey to them just how bad Lesley is feeling, but I can't. I want to take her into the hospital right now to be checked out, if only to put my mind at ease, but they talk me out of it. The nurses seem convinced she will rally soon enough and that I shouldn't worry. Though they do concede that I might want to keep them informed of Lesley's condition. Just to be on the safe side.

'She needs plenty of fluids and plenty of rest,' they remind me. I haven't forgotten, it's like a broken record spinning around my head. I just wish it was working, as Lesley tries to settle down for another fitful night's sleep.

All the concerns and confusion about the embryos are receding into the background for me now. Our little "popsicles" may be frozen up in Harley Street, but I feel even colder. Something else is growing in me, amid my frustration. Anger mixed with fear. What have they done to my wife? And what am I going to do about it? Lesley had better start feeling better pretty damn quick, or a few people are going to know about it soon enough.

3

Shutting down

I'm on a train and I have no idea where it's going. It has those old British Rail carriages you don't really see any more. No corridor, just doors at either side. Handles on the outside, no visible means of escape. There's no one else in the carriage with me and I can tell the train is speeding up. When I look down at my arms and legs I see my body fading away. Literally disappearing as the train nears its destination. I'm not surprised, because I have had this dream before. Not for a long time and it has never felt this real. But I know it well. This is my "bad train" dream, and it's at times like this that I wish I had asked some psychologist or other what it could possibly mean. I just know I have to get the hell off the train. Or stop it. Or get help from somewhere quick. Before we reach the end of the line.

Wednesday 23 May 2001
'*This is not a negotiation!*' I want to scream down the phone, but I need to stay calm. Lesley has gasped her way bravely

through an entirely wretched Tuesday and a further call to the hospital last night was met with the usual 'let's see how it goes for another day or so'.

It is clear to me that Lesley is no better this morning – in fact, she seems a whole lot worse. Her breathing is very laboured, any discomfort she had has turned into real pain, and she has now endured more than five days having barely managed to swallow a dribble of water that, even if it was wrapped up tight and chucked into the freezer, wouldn't qualify as an ice cube.

Lesley needs some help and I am in no mood to argue the toss any more. I think the nurses at the hospital have finally got the message, so I tell them we'll be there in 20 minutes. There is nothing further to discuss.

As it happens Lesley is in no fit state to travel, but we hit the road anyway and set out on the short journey to the hospital. I know she'd be sick if there was anything there to throw up, but all Lesley can manage is some dry retching and some painful moans as I tear up the country roads at breakneck pace. I try desperately not to jolt the car too much and make her feel any worse, but in reality all I can do is grit my teeth and hope for the best.

Twenty anxious minutes later I drop Lesley at the hospital door and slam my car into a parking space, before we breeze swiftly past the slightly bemused ladies at the front desk in search of someone who can actually help us. I am ready to fight anyone who gets in our way, so it is a relief to find Julia, a key member of the fertility team we trust so much, waiting for us and ready to take charge. I can see in her face that she isn't quite expecting what she sees in front of her.

Julia has probably seen or studied pretty much everything in her job, but I soon realise this is a bad one, even in her experience. A normal day in the "assisted conception" business can mean long hours, hard work, heartbreak, disappointment, embarrassment and, if you are really lucky, moments of pure joy. Today, however, is not a normal day for any of us.

We help Lesley into a chair in a conveniently empty side room and Julia summons various helpers who kick off a series of tests and try to decide on an appropriate course of action. It seems that Lesley's mild ovarian hyper-stimulation syndrome, or OHSS, is not so mild after all and has developed into something a lot more extreme. Not surprisingly, she is about as dehydrated as John Mills was just before he got his hands on the ice-cold beer in Alex, and this is everyone's immediate source of concern.

The team waste no time in putting Lesley on a saline drip, mixing in some Warfarin and Zantac for good measure. This new water and drug combo is designed to re-hydrate Lesley's bloodstream and should allow her body to recover from its current state of desiccation. It certainly seems a more efficient way of topping up her fluid levels than the old "Tommy Cooper method" we've been using up until now.

In less than two per cent of cases, Julia explains, OHSS can be very serious. Fluid collects in the stomach and chest, causing difficulty with breathing. *Tell me about it.* There is a risk of blood clots and renal problems, and in extreme cases, OHSS may become life threatening if not managed correctly.

Life threatening? I must have missed that bit in the "Preparing for IVF" manual. I'm sure it's there somewhere, but I am already beginning to realise just how unusual the situation my wife finds herself in may be.

They are very keen to take Lesley's blood pressure, but an experienced practice nurse who gives it a try finds that it has plummeted so low it is hard to get a reading. This is not something the nurse is used to and the look of frustration and concern is easy to read on her face. After three tries without success, she decides to leave it until they have found Lesley a proper hospital bed.

'Is Lesley diabetic?' one of the nurses asks me, as we transfer to another room and my wife is deposited into a bed in the hospital's high dependency area.

'Not that I know of,' I tell the nurse, rather nonplussed by the question.

The funny thing is that Lesley's blood sugar level has just hit 26. As the expected norm is around 4, this does seem a little high to everyone. Including me – and, apart from all those stress-inducing injections I have had to give Lesley recently, my only real medical experience comes from playing the game *Operation* with my brothers when I was a kid.

At least this significant blood sugar spike has given the team something else they can treat proactively. I realise I am grasping at straws here, but I feel the need to find some positives today, in the midst of the catastrophe. I observe carefully as insulin is duly added to the growing cocktail of drugs.

I am relieved that my wife is now in a place where she can be monitored carefully and looked after properly, but it is fast becoming apparent that this is not a normal situation for the nurses either.

The stock-in-trade of the private medical world is fixing people with neatly specified problems and making them better. Not bringing them back from the edge. So this situation is definitely different, and even though these things must happen from time to time around here, I'm clearly not the only one who's unsettled by what's going on in the hospital's small high dependency area today.

All that said, the medical staff here are fantastic and they can't do enough for Lesley. Karen, the doctor in charge of the fertility unit, has been on and off the phone to our consultant all morning getting instructions, and he will be here as soon as he can, probably sometime around lunch. Things are being done at last and I start to feel a little more optimistic that this whole ghastly episode could be over in the next few hours.

More good news – they finally manage to get a reading on Lesley's blood pressure. It is very low at 60 over 40, whereas a normal healthy reading would be around 120 over 80. But at least they now have something else to fill in on her chart. The high figure is known as the "systolic pressure" and this indicates the peak blood pressure in your arteries, while the lower one is the "diastolic pressure", the lowest blood pressure you hit during the resting phase of your cardiac cycle. When these two measures are really close together, as with Lesley today, you could say it makes it (please excuse the pun…) bloody hard to measure. But the nurses keep at it, every 20 minutes or so, with mixed success.

Keeping a close eye on all the vital signs is an important aspect of treating OHSS. In fact, you don't really treat the condition at all, you *manage* it. This thing is going to run its course whether we like it or not, the trick is to still have a patient when it's done. To date, very few women have ever lost their lives to OHSS, thank goodness, but that doesn't make it any more attractive a club to join.

When our fertility consultant arrives at the hospital it is fair to say he is alarmed by Lesley's weakened physical state, but he quietly assesses the situation, maintaining his familiar unflappable manner. After looking through her already copious notes covering the past few hours, he asks the nursing staff to keep at it and requests an ultra-sound scan on Lesley's liver, before heading off to attend to other matters. Lesley barely notices, she is so tired that she has been drifting in and out for a while and I keep looking for evidence that she might be perking up a little as we wait for someone to follow up on the request for the liver scan.

I'm not sure what I was expecting when I brought Lesley into the hospital this morning. A miracle cure, perhaps, or more likely some kind of exposition of Sod's Law that says by the time you actually get to see a doctor you are bound to be feeling much better. It hasn't turned out that way and by the look of the regularly updated observations on Lesley, she's not going to be leaping out of bed and getting back to her old self for quite a while.

I am beginning to realise we could be here for a long time yet, as Lesley's blood pressure remains dangerously low and her blood sugar insanely high. There's no sign of success from the rapid rehydration programme either. Despite the continual drip feeding of fluid directly into my wife's bloodstream, she's not really improving and seems as dried out and uncomfortable as ever. Where is all that liquid going, I wonder, checking the feeder tube carefully to make sure it hasn't sprung a leak.

There's no leak and the saline mixture has been steadily disappearing all day, so I'm no nearer to understanding what is happening to it. Something tells me I'm not the only one, unless someone around here is holding out on me. Perhaps the liver scan will shed some light on the situation, though I have no idea how.

What are we looking for here?, I want to ask as Lesley is loaded onto a trolley and whisked off uncomfortably to another room for the ultra-sound scan, but I can tell the wheel-'em-out-and-scan-'em team are just following orders and have no information to offer me anyway.

When we reach the scanning room, Lesley and I are expecting the compact sort of ultra-sound machine used on pregnant women and women undergoing IVF treatment as part of their regular check-ups. What we get is a heavy-duty industrial model, obviously used on all sorts of people whose predicament is so serious that an X-ray just won't cut it. As they switch on the contraption and proceed with the scan, I imagine every single dog in the local area going bananas. It must be hell for any sensitive canines who live within earshot of a maternity hospital.

It's late afternoon back in the high dependency area and I am just about dug in for the long haul when our consultant returns and hits me with a bombshell.

'Lesley is very unwell.'

'*Yes, I know.*'

'We're not really equipped to care for her properly here.'

'*Well, I was wondering about that…*'

'We are going to have to transfer her to Hammersmith.'

'*You are going to have to what?*'

'She will probably have to stay there for at least a few days. The scan shows a build-up of fluid around her liver…'

'*OK, stop right there!*' I'm losing control of the situation again and I honestly believe I'm going to start hyperventilating or something. *Hammersmith?* Neither Lesley nor I have ever been there in our lives. I know it's on our side of London and it's not really that far away, but right now it feels like we're talking about shipping Lesley off to Timbuktu. They can't do that, she's not feeling well. And she has a build-up of fluid around her liver. Apparently. *What is going on here?*

Our consultant calmly explains that they have the expertise and equipment at Queen Charlotte's Hospital in Hammersmith to handle serious OHSS cases. He has a friend from University who is based there and, having pulled a few strings, they have agreed to take Lesley. I guess it's a bit like getting into an Oxbridge college without ever having to sit the entrance exam, all because you know the right people (as if that would ever happen). I should be happy, but the implications of what I have just heard are still whizzing around my head.

First there's the prospect of a loved one being sucked into a proper hospital for what is likely to be more than just a couple of days. A *proper hospital*, equipped to deal with *proper emergencies*, full of sick and injured people, undoubtedly in a worse state than even Lesley is at this precise moment. We're both glad that these hospitals exist, hell, we're ready to get out there on the street protesting if anyone ever threatens to close one down (though we rarely have the time in our busy schedules). But we certainly don't ever want to go to one.

Then there's the practicalities of the situation to consider. How will Lesley get to Hammersmith?

'In an ambulance,' they tell me.

How will I get there? And back? When will we go? What will she need? So many questions. And how long do I have to get my head round all these logistics and to calm down a bit? I definitely need some time to decide what is so wrong with this picture. I shouldn't be so freaked out by the idea of taking Lesley somewhere she can get the best care.

I'm sitting here in a trance, people busying themselves around me, many of them attending to my stricken wife, when it hits me. This is *really happening*. It's not a dream, not an imaginary story. Not a hoax, nor a tale from a parallel world. This is real, this is our life and that actually is Lesley lying there in a hospital bed, with tubes coming out of her and her health deteriorating rapidly.

There's one thing I know for sure as I snap myself out of my torpor. We have to go to Hammersmith. For a moment I feel like Dorothy contemplating her foreboding trip along the yellow brick road. *The Wizard of Hammersmith*? Nah, it'll never fly. Especially when the road is actually the Western Avenue into central London. I last drove up and down it on Friday, on my way to the clinic on Harley Street. It's not yellow, nor is it in the least brick-like. Mostly tarmac I'd say and I don't recall traffic congestion ever being a major problem in Oz.

Thinking about it though, there is an almost palacial Art Deco buiding that looms large at the side of this not so interesting black tarmac avenue. I have seen it a few times when travelling that way through suburban Perivale, and the old Hoover Factory suddenly seems a pretty likely place for the Wizard to install his smoke and mirrors after all...

Did I mention my overactive imagination? Well, this is

another of those times when I decide it is not at all helpful. This is a moment that calls for action, so I gather myself up and head home to collect anything Lesley might need in hospital, concerned that the ambulance might arrive at any time and take her away.

I'm home and back within the hour and, as I walk inside with a bag full of useful items – toothbrush, dressing gown, nightie, change of clothes for Lesley, all stuff I am amazed I have been able to remember, let alone find – I have anxious visions of my wife having left without me. I am relieved to find her still here, awake and bewildered, but putting a brave face on the situation. We keep each other company as we wait for the ambulance and my hopes are rekindled that Lesley might just have come through the worst. Perhaps things will start to get better from here.

Almost three hours later we are still waiting for the ambulance. I realise that there was no need to panic earlier, the deadline wasn't quite as tight as I had imagined. We are relying on an NHS ambulance becoming available, so the staff at this private hospital haven't been able to give us any idea when we might be on our way. And I can tell that, as nice as they've been and as hard as they've worked, they wouldn't mind seeing the back of us sometime soon.

At last the call comes, there's a vehicle with two sturdy ambulancemen at the hospital door. Lesley describes her eager helpers as "dishy", even in her present state, and I choose to interpret this as an encouraging sign. She must be on the mend. The plan is for me to follow the ambulance, so that I have a way of getting home later. Before we leave, I have just enough time to run down to the fertility unit and thank the staff there for all their help today.

I speak briefly to whoever I can find, then finally run into Wendy, one of the team who wasn't around earlier. Now Wendy, you need to understand, is great. No-one can get a blood sample out of your arm better than she can;

she's professional and caring; she knows her job inside out just like the others – but she doesn't do subtle and is as plain speaking as they come. If you want nice, reassuring and a fantastic bedside manner, talk to pretty much anyone else from the team; if you want someone to tell you like it is, then Wendy's your girl.

So Wendy tells me like it is. When I explain that Lesley might be in hospital for a few days, she looks mildly puzzled and puts me right.

'More like weeks,' she suggests, 'certainly a couple, but be prepared for more.'

I nod stupidly, thank everyone again and wander off to my car in a bit of a daze. Weeks? This is new information I can't say I'm ready for. I file it in my tired brain for later and focus on a spot of ambulance chasing.

Well, ambulance *following* at least, but have you ever tried following an ambulance? They strut confidently through red lights flashing their "blues and twos" without so much as an "excuse me", but – and I have already been warned by the boys driving the big white bus – I can't do the same without running the risk of being pulled over by the police.

Sorry officer, I'm just following that ambulance. The one that's raced off into the distance and is now out of sight.

'Pull the other one, son, it's got bells on. You're nicked!'

Luckily, none of this happens and, for the most part, I keep up. The couple of times I lose touch with the ambulance, they are kind enough to wait for me, and it is not too long before we both pull up outside a large and imposing building on Goldhawk Road. Which is unfortunate, since it appears no one is home and I have to say I was expecting a large metropolitan hospital to be a bit busier than this. The ambulancemen are scratching their heads. This should be Queen Charlotte's Hospital. The Sat-Nav says yes, but a random passer-by tells us no. Seems that the hospital upped sticks and moved last

November, but no-one told the company who provide the ambulance's satellite navigation service. So what now?

'Du Cane Road,' offers Lesley, 'that's where they said the hospital was.'

I must have heard that earlier too, but I'll be damned if I can remember it. Even in her dehydrated, hypotensic and hyperglycemic condition, I have to admit Lesley still does detail so much better than me. Relieved to have some kind of lead on their destination, the ambulancemen plot a course. Du Cane Road is less than three miles away, we'll be there within minutes...

And we are. At Queen Charlotte's and Chelsea Hospital, to be precise, rehoused just six months ago in its brand new building at the Hammersmith Hospital. To be fair, it was on Goldhawk Road for almost 160 years, so we didn't miss it by very much.

I have to say though, on first impressions this place doesn't look much more lively than the one it replaced. But it is almost 9.30 at night, so I shouldn't be expecting thronging crowds and a grand welcome. It takes quite a while for the ambulancemen to drum up any interest from inside, but finally Lesley is aboard yet another trolley and is trundling into the building. I am at her side, as we whip up a dimly lit corridor, turn left, turn right, take a short ride in a lift and then, rather unexpectedly, find ourselves in a private room. At which point, our entire medical entourage leaves us alone for what seems forever, and I have the opportunity to assess our new surroundings.

Great, we've got a telly, I think, forgetting everything for a moment and switching it on to catch the last few minutes of the football. It's the Champions League Final tonight between Bayern Munich and Valencia at the San Siro stadium in Milan. The game is deadlocked at 1-1, low in energy, with chances few and far between. Lesley and I have had that sort of day too, and it looks like we're all in for extra time of some kind or another.

When the nurses reappear, they resume the same routine we have become familiar with today.

'Are you diabetic?' they ask Lesley.

'*Has this woman actually got any blood pressure at all?*' they wonder to themselves.

The observations are just as regular, but they don't get any easier, and now Lesley is really starting to look pretty out of it. We wait for the duty doctor, who eventually comes and goes with little to say. He fits a catheter, which seems to add to rather than relieve Lesley's discomfort. We console ourselves with the knowledge that the chief consultant will be round in the morning and he will know what to do to fix all this.

The evening stretches on. Lesley rests uncomfortably, Bayern win 5-4 on penalties and finally a nurse comes by to kick me out. Goodbyes are predictably tearful and I still can't believe I am leaving Lesley here tonight. I'm not sure if I even know exactly where *here* is. But I have to leave now and I do, knowing that I'll be back in the morning after as much sleep I can manage.

I feel numb as I drive away from the hospital and hit the road out of London, finding it very hard to accept everything that has happened. Suddenly tired, I jab on the radio to hear some late night chatter about rising gun crime on Radio 5 Live. It's heavy stuff after the day I've had and I can't concentrate on it at all. If I had my Elvis Costello CDs in the car he would be singing to me as I drive through Perivale. Doesn't matter, his voice is in my head anyway.

The song is spookily appropriate, as he's singing about the Western Avenue out of London and 'the splendour of the Hoover Factory'. Two lines in particular bring a lump to my throat:

'*It's not a matter of life or death, but what is, what is?*
It doesn't matter if I take another breath. Who cares,
who cares?'

I wonder if my old mate *The Wizard of Hammersmith* cares? I doubt it, but I can't help giving him a little wave as I drive past his house. Just in case.

4

Hammersmith

I had never really thought about just how smart the human body is. It knows when to breathe, it knows how to break down the air it receives into useful stuff like oxygen, and it knows what to do with it when it gets it. It can process all kinds of foodstuffs or beverages, and with the minimum of fuss it distributes nutrients and water to wherever they're needed. My heart beats maybe 80 times per minute on a good day, pumping blood neatly around my veins and through my vital organs, with very little of it ever coming out, short of a particularly bad nosebleed I can remember or an accident with a kitchen knife that I hope will never happen. It does all of these things and much more without me ever needing to ask it. Good thing really, because if anyone ever switched off the autopilot and my body had to rely on me to give it instructions, I'd probably be dead within the hour.

Thursday 24 May 2001
I wake up just after 6am and lie here for a moment, while

my brain does its best to catch up with my body. The room is silent as I stretch out an arm and realise Lesley is not here.

Yesterday wasn't a dream, even if it seems like one now. The whole day flashes through my mind and it's still a blur. The house, the hospital, the ambulance, another much bigger hospital, then somehow back to the house. I don't even remember getting home.

What do I need to do today? Go to the hospital obviously, but what else? Our life is supposed to have continued this week, but things have come to an unscheduled stop. I need to pick up the threads, tie them together and get control of the situation, even if only temporarily. The first of these threads is a whole series of phone calls I have to make to Lesley's family, starting with her dad. I go for a certain amount of sugaring of the pill when I explain what has happened, as I don't want to scare him or any of the family unduly. I certainly don't want to let any of them know how terrified I am myself at this moment.

Visiting Lesley's work is my next task of the morning. She is in the middle of a big project, designing a heavy industrial tools catalogue for a newly formed offshoot of the company she works for. Lesley is the only one there who has mastered the dark arts of the devilishly difficult but very powerful desktop publishing program they are using, so the project is just a tad dependent on her involvement at this stage. The company's small office is just round the corner from home, so I swing by and give them the bad news that all their eager heavy industrial tool users may have to wait a little bit longer to order their professional-grade grinders, specialist drill attachments and other suitably destructive or creative items.

Lesley's bosses take it remarkably well. So I am pleased to put a tick in this particular box without mishap, and will carry all the best wishes of Lesley's colleagues to her later this morning.

What else? Oh no – Ellen! Lesley's pal from back home in Manchester is coming down to see us tomorrow. The plan is for her to come for the whole of next week, relax for a few days, go out and do stuff. Fun stuff. What am I going to tell her? Fun seems to be off the agenda for the foreseeable future, unless hospital visiting floats Ellen's particular boat.

I need to call her so she can cancel her trip until Lesley's feeling better. When I reach Ellen with the news that there is a problem with Lesley, she asks me if my better half has been baking again and I can hear the smile in her voice. This is not the reaction I was expecting and it takes me a moment or two to understand the reference…

OK, I'm there. A few months ago, the last time I called Ellen in fact, I had expressed my concern for Lesley.

'What's wrong?' Ellen's voice was filled with anguish.

'She's started baking cakes,' I explained. 'How weird is that?'

During almost fourteen years of marriage this had never happened before. It was a whim, a fancy, nothing to worry about at all, but I had to go and wind up Lesley's friend. Ellen, by the way, can bake a mean cake herself and regularly whips up a range of tasty desserts, so I knew she'd appreciate the joke. At the time.

Now, of course, the joke is on me.

'Ah no, it's not the baking this time, it's a bit more serious.'

I tell Ellen what's happened and suggest we reschedule her visit. She is hearing none of it. If Ellen could possibly board a train right this minute I believe she would, but she tells me she'll be down on Friday as planned. The week ahead may not promise the fun-filled relaxing vacation she had been expecting, but Ellen will be there for Lesley – always has been, always will be.

I call into my work around 10 o'clock, update them on the situation and walk around the office a bit talking to people, trying to introduce a bit of normality back into my life. I even check my work emails. Completely pointless, as I have no intention of replying to any of them. It's not quite 10.15 when I realise that I am postponing the inevitable trip to Hammersmith and, of course, I am desperate – if a little scared – to find out how Lesley is doing this morning.

My head is prepared for the journey and I have already worked out a direct route from here straight down the M1, then around the North Circular to the hospital. My heart, however, is pounding fifteen to the dozen. I find it strangely difficult to imagine that I can actually find the hospital in the cold light of day – especially since the ambulance driver had all that trouble last night.

But I do, and it's surprisingly easy. The only real problem I have is finding somewhere to park. Most UK hospitals these days have introduced a new local taxation system to help with funding, in the form of hefty parking fees. Hammersmith doesn't have that luxury, as they don't even have a car park.

Scouring Du Cane Road for somewhere to leave the car I struggle to find a gap, as the whole area is just a teensy bit busier this morning than last night. When I do find a space, it is some distance up the road and is pretty much opposite the prison gates of Wormwood Scrubs. I wince as I notice the parking ticket machine nearby is broken. It is hard not to imagine that this is the result of some hardened ex-con taking his revenge on the system that put him away. By breaking the parking ticket machine? Well, maybe not that hardened then, but it must have felt good.

Frustrated and a little unsure what to do next I allow the atmosphere around the place opposite to pervade my mood. I decide to buck the parking authorities myself, as the nearest ticket machine is probably miles away. Obviously I am not that brave, so I leave a little note on my windscreen: 'Parking ticket machine broken.' If it's good enough for TV's most celebrated cockney wideboy "Del

Boy" Trotter, then it's good enough for me.

Suitably puffed up by my act of rebellion I head for the hospital and quickly search out Lesley's room. She is resting quietly, but is in severe discomfort. I am so relieved to see her, but I grow wary as I realise there is a visible change in Lesley, even since last night. She is still on a drip, and is being pumped regularly with various medications through a sore-looking vein in her hand. Her breathing is worse and she now has access to an oxygen mask whenever she needs it.

But the thing I really can't help noticing is the swelling in many parts of her body. Fluid build up, I am informed. Lesley has put on some three or four stones of weight in the last 24 hours. In fact, most of the liquid that has been dripping into her body since I took her into hospital yesterday has been going to all the wrong places. We knew about the build-up around Lesley's liver from the scan yesterday, but it now looks like all her major organs are being crushed by the weight of the liquid the doctors and nurses have so diligently pushed into her body.

This is ovarian hyper-stimulation syndrome at its most vindictive. Lesley is in desperate need of re-hydration – her whole body, the organs, the blood, her muscles and soft tissue are all screaming for water. Meanwhile, fluid is floating around her system in big pools, somehow being directed by the OHSS to sit around and observe the biggest problems (in most of Lesley's vital organs), but on no account to help out. I can only suggest that they take Lesley off the drip before it gets any worse, but they can't. The drip is the lesser of two evils. If they take it away, the dehydration's going to do for her long before the OHSS can.

I ask Lesley if she has seen the main consultant, but she's not sure. More than one doctor has passed through here this morning, all with some degree of specialist knowledge in the treatment of her condition. One of them may have been the big white-coated chief, but it is hard for her to tell. Lesley is now subject to a strict regimen of medical observations and changing shifts of nursing staff have disturbed her at half-hour intervals throughout the night. Deprived of food, water and sleep by the OHSS in this way, it is entirely predictable that Lesley's oft proven powers of retaining all the details might finally start to fail her.

I was hoping to see the chief consultant myself, but I make up for it by grilling every doctor I see. What I learn at first is minimal and of dubious value to us, but I'm a persistent so-and-so when I want to be. They soon realise there is no point in resisting my interrogations and they answer my questions as courteously as they can during the course of the day.

So, in case you were wondering, OHSS is the most common serious side effect of ovarian stimulation using drugs called "gonadotrophins", a word which I have to admit sounds a lot funnier when you say it slowly. And yes, our old friend Puragon is indeed a gonadotrophin, a very potent one. What it does is push your ovaries so hard that it makes a US army trainee's life in *Full Metal Jacket* look like a walk in the park. The desired payoff is the production of several eggs, but the downside is that the ovaries they spring from are highly likely to swell. And even a slight enlargement of the ovaries can bring on OHSS.

Unsurprisingly then, this is a very common after-effect of fertility treatment. There is a general feeling of bloating and some pain in the abdomen. As a man I can barely guess how this feels, but I am sure that it would keep me off work for at least a week. I suspect most women in this situation simply dismiss it as a minor discomfort, certainly no worse than bad period pains.

For a tiny percentage of sufferers, however, OHSS gets a lot nastier. In its moderate form you can mix in nausea, vomiting, diarrhoea and breathlessness. All common enough symptoms that most people suffer from at times, but particularly unpleasant when gathered together. If it stops there you can muddle through. *Plenty of fluids, plenty of rest and you'll be fine in a few days.*

Doesn't always stop there, though.

In a few very rare cases, it gets worse and when you hit "severe" on the OHSS-ometer, it's time to start reaching out for the medical dictionary. Typically, if the ovaries swell to more than 12 centimetres in size you get what are known as "clinical ascites". This means that fluid is accumulating in the cavities around the liver – not a good sign and something that normally only happens when the patient is suffering from cirrhosis and severe liver disease. Next up is "hydrothorax", a condition arising from a similar fluid build-up, this time around the lungs. There is also increased blood viscosity and electrolyte disturbance, which probably go a fair way to explaining Lesley's extremely low blood pressure. Next, a whole bunch of hypos come into play, such as "hypoproteinaemia" and "hypovolaemia". Respectively, that's a dangerously low level of protein in your blood and a general lack of blood altogether.

If I thought my head was spinning before, then trying to take all this in has just about pushed me off the scale. But I need to stay calm. I have to stay in control. At least I know something about what's going on now and I try to compose myself as I hear another of those little whispers in my ear. Rather bizarrely, it seems to come from some kind of ethereal version of Chris Tarrant in customary game show mode.

'Severe OHSS. Now that's yours. Take a look at it. Hold it…but we don't want to give you that!' he tells me.

'Try this one for "critical" – is it (a) a large hydrothorax with haematocrit, (b) a thrombo-embolism, (c) Adult Respiratory Distress Syndrome, or (d) hypercoagulability?'

'*Do I really have to play, Chris?*'

'Yes.'

'*Can I phone a friend?*'

'No.'

'*Bugger.*'

I really have no idea what most of this stuff means, but thrombo-embolism? That's a bad thing for sure. In fact, the doctors tell me it's worse than bad, being a not-so-neat little cocktail of deep vein thrombosis (DVT) and a pulmonary embolism.

Very bad then.

Not that any of the other stuff sounds any better. They are all things I can barely pronounce, let alone understand. And if Lesley isn't suffering from them now, she may well have them to look forward to.

'*Cheers Chris, you can get lost now.*'

Come later in the evening I have enough medical details to start work on a dissertation and the doctors have left us in no doubt we are dealing with critical OHSS here. Even here at Hammersmith, unquestionably the number one place in the country to be with this kind of problem, critical OHSS is hardly run-of-the-mill stuff. In fact, the doctors here have seen only one similar case in the past six years. I'll say one thing for Lesley, she sure knows how to stand out in the crowd.

My wife has also managed to keep her spirits up remarkably well considering, but she is entitled to some grumpiness. Her situation has not improved at all today and the room is starting to close in on us both. At least they've sorted out the dodgy catheter, but Lesley is hardly any more comfortable tonight.

It is time for me to leave and there's still no sign of the main consultant. I have discovered he was around first thing this morning and he won't be back until tomorrow. Nobody knows exactly when. I am keen to speak to him, but I am even keener on keeping close tabs on Lesley. I have found a phone in her room, so it doesn't seem unreasonable for me to call her. No problem, the nurses tell me and I make a note of the number.

The line carries a premium charge, but like the victim of any successful scam, I really don't care at this point. I am also relieved to think that I can pass the number on to Lesley's dad and other members of her family, so that they can speak to her too.

Despite my attempts to sanitise the horrors of the last couple of days, I know they have all been out of their minds with worry since hearing the news. Tonight as I leave, I am reassured by the fact that we all have a way of contacting Lesley any time we want, within reason, and the drive home feels a little less lonely for it.

5

Ellen

When I was a kid I had a very special friend. His name was Gooder, and he even had a few friends of his own who turned up from time to time, like Goodie and the Wizard. Rather peculiarly, Gooder was only a few inches tall and he lived under the kitchen sink. I seem to recall he looked a bit like a leprechaun, although it was hard to tell because he was invisible. My younger brother Richard never liked him. Jealous I guess. One day Richard came up to me and proudly announced that he had just hit Gooder. Naturally, I gave my brother a damn good hiding. We were only three and four years old at the time, but no one hurts my friends. I'd have done anything for that little fella under the sink. And I'd like to think he'd have been there for me too. That's what friends are for.

Friday 25 May 2001

I have my daily routine worked out already. Call Lesley first thing on the premium hospital phone line to make sure she's OK. Or at least to make sure that she is whatever passes for "OK" at the moment. Next, drop into work and mope around for a bit looking miserable, before heading for Hammersmith around mid-morning.

With the car slotted neatly into another "free" space at the roadside opposite the gates of the Scrubs, I make my way shiftily towards Queen Charlotte's. Passing the broken ticket machine, I am silently aware that I may be the fool who rushed in where the local parking inspectors fear to tread, but what the heck, it worked for me yesterday. I find Lesley in her room, two stones or more worth of fluid heavier. How is she coping with this? It's like something out of a science fiction film – she's been invaded by some kind of alien creature, and it's growing inside her.

The irony of this bizarre parallel with an actual pregnancy arising from our disastrous IVF cycle is not lost on me, but I decide not to mention it.

I ask about the consultant. Lesley says that he has been around and she is expecting him to reappear later this afternoon. The other doctors and nurses have been in and out, of course, and Lesley has already singled out one nurse for a special place in hell. Not that she's necessarily a bad person or anything, actually she's been caring for my wife every step of the way since we arrived at Queen Charlotte's. But she does have a habit of pushing and poking Lesley around when she wants to move her. And it really hurts. Of course, just about every movement hurts now. This is the kind of situation the polite request 'handle with care' could have been written for.

The trouble is, Lesley wanted to have a shower this morning and the enemy nurse was the only one around to help. Having been told 'no' several times, and that she really wasn't up to it, Lesley finally convinced the nurse that it was worth a try. So, armed with a walking frame and her sceptical nurse guide, my wife made a brave attempt to trek the five-foot trail across the room to the en-suite shower cubicle.

And she made it! Just.

Mindful of allowing Lesley some small amount of dignity, the nurse duly left her to it for a couple of minutes. Unfortunately, a shower is not the easiest thing to cope with when you are struggling to stand, walk or even move much at all. By the time the nurse returned Lesley had collapsed in the cubicle, managed to crawl back across the room and was lying slumped on her bed, wet through. As she tells me the tale, Lesley has to concede that the nurse may have called this one right all along. I just marvel at my wife's resilience and the fact that she can retain such a level head when faced with all this adversity.

One of the doctors pops by to see how Lesley is and tells us there's a problem with the line into her hand. This is important as the line is a feeder tube delivering all manner of medications and magic bean extracts directly into her vein, along with the continuous drip of fluid that is maintaining and threatening her body's organs, all at the same time. We can see that the line is not wearing well after a couple of days, in fact it seems to have seized up completely and the bruising around the insertion looks very angry indeed. Lesley's veins are not the most co-operative at the best of times, right now they are in a particularly belligerent frame of mind.

Apparently, the consultant decided earlier this morning that the feeder tube will have to go, but that only really leaves one viable alternative.

'A central line will be better anyway,' explains the doctor.

Fine with me, Lesley's sore hand needs a break from all the pressure and a "central line" sounds innocuous enough. Until I ask what it is.

Perhaps I am a little naïve when it comes to medical matters, or maybe I just haven't spent enough Saturday nights glued to BBC1's latest episode of *Casualty*, but finding out what a central line is comes as something of a shock. What they do is poke a hole in your neck with a scalpel, then force a small plastic tube down your main artery until it reaches your heart. Everything you need – medication, fluid, chicken soup maybe? – is then delivered via this central line, meaning that it is introduced into your bloodstream much quicker and more efficiently than is possible by burdening some solitary little vein with all the responsibility.

I watch them do it and it's horrible. Hoisted up, so that she is almost upside-down, Lesley has the tube pushed into her neck and it is forced down as far as it will go. I wonder how they know when to stop? The whole thing strikes me as an over elaborate method of stabbing someone in the heart, worthy of the most ingenious serial killer. On the sly, I double-check the doctor's nametag, if only to reassure myself that I can eliminate Hannibal Lecter and Harold Shipman from my list of suspects.

It is beginning to dawn on me just how much of a nightmare our adventures into the fun and happening world of fertility treatment have landed us in. Or rather, just how much of a nightmare they have landed Lesley in – as she is the one who seems to be at the business end of this particularly cruel medical experiment gone wrong. None of this should be happening, I tell myself. And, in 99 point lots more 9s per cent of the time it wouldn't be – Lesley's predicament is the very definition of "cruel and unusual". Tough break, but here we are.

The hospital has a quiet hour each day between 2 and 3 o'clock in the afternoon, and visitors have to make themselves scarce. As diligent in my visiting duties as I am trying to be, I have to confess the break is welcome.

Today though, I have another purpose. I need to go to Watford. Lesley's friend Ellen is on the Manchester train arriving at Watford Junction around 4 o'clock, so I need to get my skates on to meet her. Fortunately, it's not a difficult journey at this time of day and I make it with something to spare. It's great to see her and, having negotiated a slightly choked up greeting, I grab Ellen's bag and sling it in the car.

When I suggest we head home so she can freshen up, she insists we drive straight to Hammersmith. Ellen can't wait to see her pal. I can only hope she is ready for what she's about to see when we get to the hospital.

We chat on the way. Small talk mainly. Ellen hates travelling at night, that's why she had always planned to take Friday off work and travel down during the day. She reminds me that we were all going to see *The Witches of Eastwick* in the West End of London on Wednesday. That's not looking all that likely right now, short of a pact with the devil, which feels somewhat appropriate but is probably a stretch even for me.

I try to explain a little bit of what has happened over the last few days, but it is hard to know where to start. While I have been keeping some of our family and friends up to date with events, it occurs to me that I haven't really let anyone into the *Twilight Zone* Lesley and I are currently inhabiting. Letting Ellen in on what we are going through right now is a big thing. For us and for her. I feel guilty. This is not what Ellen signed up for when we arranged her visit. Lesley is suffering and it's my burden. It's my job to fix this somehow, no one else's.

I can't expect Ellen to go through all this with us. Not again.

The last time we dragged Ellen into related if not quite similar circumstances was just a few months ago. Back then, Lesley and I were waiting to see whether our first go at IVF had been successful. It coincided with a long-planned break in the North East of England and Ellen was sharing a holiday cottage with us, on the outskirts of Costa del Gateshead. When Lesley confirmed that she wasn't pregnant it put a bit of a downer on the week, but hey, we saw the Angel of the North and Lindisfarne Island – what more could you want? We even experienced the nightlife of Newcastle city centre and went shopping in the Metro Centre, so I'm sure Ellen still has some happy memories of the trip...

Our first IVF was actually our third treatment cycle at our local private hospital. Initially the team there had suggested we try a thing called IUI, also known as "intra-uterine insemination". It's a similar thing, although a whole lot simpler than IVF – but it has more of the farmyard than the posh fertility clinic about it. IUI involves relatively gentle doses of drugs to regulate a woman's natural ovulation cycle, plus a fresh sperm sample, one of these handy centrifuge machines and what amounts to a turkey baster. The unsuspecting sperm are spun and sorted for purity, as is usual during an IVF cycle, then only the most rampant warriors among them are sent off to do their work, just as an egg is expected to appear on a nearby ovary.

IUI relies on an egg actually being produced and a healthy slice of luck, upping the chances of conception from the natural next-to-no-chance to all of about five per cent. Needless to say, neither of our IUI attempts worked out. They were a mere warm-up for what was to come anyway – we kind of knew that all along. So when our consultant at the fertility unit suggested we move onto the more hardcore world of IVF, with greatly enhanced prospects of success, we jumped at the chance. Had we realised that the road would be this rocky and that it would lead all the way to Hammersmith, we might have been more reluctant to take it.

When Ellen and I reach the hospital, the least I can do for her is try to avoid the prison gates, so I find a spot for the car much nearer to Queen Charlotte's itself and pay at the ticket machine as if this is the most normal thing in the world for me. We hurry inside and find Lesley's room. She is delighted to see her friend and there are tears on both sides.

I notice that Ellen is quiet. She says and does all the right things, but she is subdued. I understand. There is a lot for her to take in here. Lesley's physical condition is a shock in itself. The fluid build-up is extraordinary, especially if you haven't been there to see how it has progressed over the last few days. She looks pale and weak, her breathing is shallow and she speaks in a strained whisper. Everything she does has to be very deliberate and requires a great deal of effort. On top of that, Lesley has the central line sticking not at all prettily out of her neck, an oxygen mask over her mouth, and she is the proud wearer of a fetching pair of those stockings that guard against the danger of blood clots and deep vein thrombosis.

Ellen handles the scene with all the calmness and grace I have been lacking over the last few days. I still feel guilty about pulling her into all this, but I am grateful for her support. I can see that Lesley is too. It is a relief for her to see another friendly face, and it is good for us both to have someone else around who is not preoccupied with taking Lesley's body temperature, blood pressure or measuring her blood sugar levels every half hour or so.

The three of us are quite settled when one of the nurses whispers that the chief consultant is on his way. It feels like we're at school and someone has just warned us that the teacher is coming. Ellen and I need to put away our marbles and *Top Trumps* cards quickly and pretend we are just checking through last night's algebra homework. We are silent as Mr Margara sweeps into the room with that air of supreme over-confidence we demand of all our top physicians. He is like a force of nature and has in train an entourage comprising all the doctors I have seen around the place for the past couple of days.

The boss man immediately wants to know who I am and when he identifies me as the husband, a shrug indicates that I can stay as long as I behave. Ellen he shoos away, dismissing her after hearing that she is merely

Lesley's friend with the simple challenge, 'and what are you still doing here?'

I am aghast. Ellen is open mouthed, but she takes it in her stride and walks out of the room without a word. There will be some choice ones later, of that I am sure.

Raul Margara is one of those larger than life people you encounter from time to time. Not actually scary, but he can knock you off your stride with practised ease. He is also one of the most respected consultants in his field, so I'm pleased to see him here, even if his entrance has cast me as a nervous Simon Sparrow against his Lancelott Spratt from one of those 1950s *Doctor in the House* films.

The medical conference around Lesley's bed lasts no more than a few minutes. Naturally I am in the thick of it, keen not to miss anything, but there is very little new to learn. A whole host of OHSS symptoms are mentioned and these are showing no signs of going away. The doctors think that they have some degree of control over Lesley's condition for now, but it's a tricky balancing act.

Mr Margara's final words to Lesley before he leaves to continue his rounds hang in the room for quite some time.

'You're in for a rough weekend.'

6

The rough weekend

They tell me it's another warm day out there. I have no way to be sure, because I can't see or feel anything outside of my bubble any more. I keep punching the wall, but it makes no difference. My hands are red raw, yet blue with the cold. When I cough, I can see my breath and the thick ice walls of my prison are closing in on me. The really stupid thing is that I knew I was going to end up somewhere like this. Some smug little know-it-all part of my gut kept telling me there was a dark shape on the horizon. I barely caught a glimpse of it from a long way off and it scared me half to death even then. Up close, it's far worse than I could ever have feared and it seems futile to imagine there is any way out of this place now. Why didn't I just stop things when I still could?

Saturday 26 May 2001
The weekend doesn't mean that much to me right now, but at least there's no need to worry about making another hollow appearance at work today.

Ellen has decided she will only come to the hospital with me every other day. It makes sense and I'm fairly sure her decision has nothing to do with the fact that Mr Margara might in any way have wound her up with his welcome yesterday. Unfazed this morning, she brushes aside her encounter with our chief consultant over a bowl of Weetabix and plans a quiet day at our house.

I grab the phone to call Lesley, but the line just rings out, no answer. I'm guessing that she's been dragged off to the toilet or something, even though when I stop to think about it, that makes very little sense. Perhaps if I leave it for 10 minutes...

Still no answer.

It's the same when I try a couple more times.

'What the hell is going on?' I ask the telephone handset.

I mean, Lesley's phone is right by her bed. She must be able to hear it. Why doesn't she pick up? *What...the hell...*

This is one of those moments in my life when I imagine the worst possible scenario, double it, add a couple of noughts and then spend 10 minutes or so fighting off a panic attack, while desperately pleading with my brain to come up with a highly plausible reason why whatever else I'm thinking is nonsense.

OK, so Lesley is not picking up the phone. There could be many explanations why a woman who can barely move, let alone walk, appears to have wandered off.

'The nurses may have whisked her off for some test or other,' a voice inside my brain chips in.

'*It's possible.*'

'The phone may be on the blink.'

'*Could be.*'

'Perhaps she simply can't hear the phone.'

'*I've already thought of that. It's right by her bed, stupid.*'

I'm unable to come up with a satisfactory explanation for Lesley's radio silence, so I scrabble around for the ward sister's phone number at the hospital. I have written it down somewhere for just this kind of emergency. Ellen helps me to look, but we're both at a bit of loss. I know I jotted down the number the night Lesley and I arrived at Queen Charlotte's, but the details of that evening are already a little hazy. What did I do with it?

Clearing my head, I try to engage some kind of autopilot in my subconscious that might let me Google the information I need in the three dimensions of my house. I find myself drawn to the jacket I was wearing that night at the hospital. Filed not so efficiently in one of the pockets I find a crumpled scrap of paper with a barely legible phone number hastily scrawled on it.

My elation quickly turns into a faint queasiness as I pick up the phone again. I punch in the number before my courage deserts me and am lucky enough to reach the ward sister first time. I have barely mumbled my name and a brief hello, when I blurt out: 'Where's Lesley?'

The answer is as matter of fact as you like.

'They've taken her down to High Dependency.'

'Right. And?'

'And they've taken her down to High Dependency.'

Stunned, I pause for a moment and try to think of that one incisive and highly intelligent question that's going to help me understand exactly what she's telling me. There is a tremble in my voice and all I manage is: 'Why?'

'Well, they can look after her better there than in the Intensive Care Unit.'

Intensive Care Unit? OK, so this conversation is not going anywhere I actually want it to go, but I persist.

It seems that Lesley was moved from her room on the ward early this morning. The Intensive Care Unit was seriously considered, as her physical condition continued to deteriorate overnight. On balance, however, the doctors in charge decided that the specialist care available on the High Dependency Ward would be better suited to helping Lesley through the rough weekend ahead.

The telephone handset is still hanging in the air, like something out of a *Roadrunner* cartoon, as I jump in my car and cover the 30 or so miles to Queen Charlotte's Hospital in record time. The woman on the front desk directs me to Lesley's new location and I race off up the corridor to find her.

When I get there, my wife is in an open ward in a bay with just two beds opposite one another and its own exclusive nursing station. A functional environment, just one step short of intensive care, has replaced the apparent luxury of her previous en-suite bedroom. Even the bed Lesley is now in has been specially hired from another medical facility, and comes with the capability to adjust, tip and tilt in all manner of useful ways. It's a fabulous toy for the hospital staff, but it is also invaluable when your mobility is severely affected by a critical illness.

Lesley's oxygen mask has become pretty much a permanent fixture, she just lifts it off her face for a few moments to speak or cough, or simply because it has become really irritating and she needs a break.

I have also noticed a new adornment to Lesley's collection of medical accessories. She now has a tube coming out of her nose, which snakes down into a second plastic bag at the side of her bed to accompany the ever-present catheter bag. It's all very *punk rock*, but I'm thinking that the removal of excess levels of snot is probably not our priority here. In fact, the tube extends all the way down Lesley's throat and into her stomach. She knows it is there to drain off excess bile and acid, but she can barely remember it being pushed in. This I suspect is one small mercy as, even if it wasn't a painful procedure, it must have been extremely unpleasant.

Concern levels among the doctors have gone up just a notch or two overnight, as they have determined that one of Lesley's lungs has effectively collapsed under the pressure of the intense fluid build-up. The other lung is not faring too well either and several other organs are in significant danger. Her body is now carrying more than seven stones of fluid that shouldn't be there. The effect is devastating. We have just about reached the limits of my wife's physical endurance and there is much debate among the doctors about the most effective strategy from here.

They are reluctant to perform further intrusive procedures to alleviate the problem, as Lesley has suffered enough and they really don't want any more complications. Their best hope is that this is a low point, and that her body will fight back on its own from here. The doctors decide to give it another 24 hours before taking more drastic action to tackle the fluid build-up. And even then, they will probably hold off if they see some improvement in Lesley's condition.

Sunday 27 May 2001

Twenty-four hours later, there is no improvement. Lesley barely looks like the same person I brought into the hospital just four days ago. The sparkle in her eyes has dimmed and I can see her fading in front of me. I have never felt as sad, frightened and completely, utterly helpless in my life. There's nothing I can do except hope that some bright spark around here can come up with something that will turn this whole thing around. Very soon.

Ellen has travelled to Hammersmith with me today and more than ever I am glad of her support. My mum and dad are coming up to visit Lesley too. They caught a train to London from the south coast earlier and I'm expecting them around lunchtime. How they will handle the sight of their naturally loud and lively daughter-in-law in her current state, I really don't know. Something tells me they couldn't have picked a more disturbing day to visit the hospital and I fear that what they see this afternoon may haunt them both for some time.

For now though, I'm just concerned with tracking down

one of the doctors to ask them what they're going to do and when. One of the team has mentioned the possibility of fitting a chest drain to relieve the pressure on Lesley's organs. Wise after Friday's central line event, I am under no illusions that this will be any more pleasant than trying to cut your toenails with a chainsaw – but judging by what I see in front of me today, the alternative could be much worse.

I am certain that Lesley's body has swelled with at least another stone of fluid since yesterday and when I do catch up with a doctor, she has grim news. The medical staff believe that Lesley's one "good" lung is now running at something like a quarter of full capacity. If we don't see some small signs of recovery right away… well, I don't even want to think about it.

They have decided to fit the chest drain and the call is out for someone to come and do the procedure. It's fairly straightforward stuff but gruesome, and I am not surprised to learn that it involves stabbing Lesley with a scalpel, then sticking another tube inside her. This tends to be how things get done around here. I am in no position to argue.

Unfortunately, my parents arrive just minutes before we are expecting Mack the Knife to turn up and do his thing. There is barely time for them to say hello to Lesley and for me to register the shock in their faces, before we are ushered away from my wife's bedside. The scene on Higher Dependency is all a bit too much for my mum and she is in tears as Ellen, my parents and I retreat to the patients' and visitors' rest room, some twenty paces down the corridor. We try to make ourselves comfortable, sitting on those odd chairs with very firm cushions that you only seem to come across in hospitals or doctors' surgeries.

And we wait.

If you've ever seen that scene in *Reservoir Dogs* where Michael Madsen's character has a policeman tied to a chair and gets to work torturing him, then you may have some idea what sitting in the rest room feels like for us. The truly horrifying stuff all happens off camera, but it's the screaming that gets to you.

When it is all over, I return to the ward on my own to find Lesley sobbing with some messy gauze and tape stuck to her side, holding a tube in position that I have to assume is the much heralded chest drain. The doctor who fitted it has already gone, so in the absence of anyone to hit, I sit next to my wife and try to console her.

'That was agony,' Lesley tells me through gritted teeth.

She walks me through the nightmare of the past few minutes, explaining how it took the doctor three attempts before he got it right. That's three sharp stabs in her side, with the merest hint of local anaesthetic. He managed to numb the surface of Lesley's skin before getting busy with the scalpel, but there is very little anyone can do to ease the pain in the muscle and fatty tissue underneath. Each time the doctor thought he had made the hole he wanted, he tried to force the tube deep inside, through Lesley's rib cage and into her chest cavity. By the third attempt, the pain was excruciating and she is at least relieved that this part of her torture has finally ended.

I look down at the side of Lesley's bed. The catheter and bile bags have been joined by a third now, this one hanging from the new tube in Lesley's side. I am a little heartened to see that the new bag is filling up nicely.

There is a bizarre symmetry to all this. Hanging from a stand at the side of the bed is yet another bag connected by a tube to Lesley's neck, dripping fluid into her dangerously dehydrated body. Much of this we now know is exiting her bloodstream at the first opportunity and gathering in pools like the one weighing heavy on her chest. Now, by the miracles of modern science, some of this liquid is being siphoned out of her chest via a similar tube and ending its journey in an identical bag hanging at the other side of her bed. It's like recycling on a human level, but if anyone so much as suggests we can save a couple of quid by running one of these bags of liquid through the central line a second time, I'm going to smash their face in.

After just half an hour, the bag attached to the chest drain has filled up with brownish, slightly bloodstained fluid and the nurses remove it and swap it for a new one. I watch carefully as they take the old bag away and dispose of it. This has to be a good sign and Lesley is buoyed up by the news.

I decide it is time to fetch our guests and everyone sits down for a nice civilised chat in the middle of the High Dependency Ward, the way we tend to do in England when everything is falling apart around us. Preferably with a cup of tea in hand.

By the time they leave the hospital, my mum and dad have seen a tiny bit of the sparkle that normally characterises their daughter-in-law. It is just enough to reassure them after the horrors of the day, but my parents are still visibly shaken as I walk them to the front door of the building.

'She's not going to let this beat her,' my dad reassures me – he has seen the strength and determination that is keeping Lesley going through all this.

Mum and Dad's visit has meant a lot to me today, but all I can do now is smile weakly and thank them for coming, choking on my words as we say our goodbyes. Aside from Ellen, who is part of all this now whether she likes it or not, my parents have been Lesley's first visitors at Queen Charlotte's. It really hasn't gone too badly, given all the stabbing and the screaming, and the general unpleasantness, the worst of which I dearly hope is over.

I think it may be time to allow a few more visitors to come up here. Lots of people have asked me about it. They have sent enough cards and flowers to fill the whole ward, and a couple more besides. Lesley is really keen for them to come, but it all depends on whether she is up to it.

As the afternoon turns into evening, Ellen and I talk to Lesley and do our best to lift her spirits. The chest drain is certainly working. I have no doubt that for now there is more liquid coming out of my wife's body than is going in via the drip. This has to help, but it is such a small thing that it makes very little difference to her overall comfort levels. I remind myself that Lesley hasn't eaten for more than a week, her blood pressure is still dragging along the floor, the risk of a blood clot due to deep vein thrombosis remains very real while her mobility is so restricted, and she continues to gasp for breath on account of having the use of about a quarter of a single lung.

Lesley has had better days, but my hopes are higher tonight. This morning was the lowest point since the false joy of the egg retrieval some nine or so days ago, and for the first time, I have seen a very small improvement in Lesley's condition. It's so tiny that you would need a very high-powered microscope to see it properly, yet I convince myself it's there. The doctors remain cautious, but I know Lesley is fighting back and I really believe she has turned a corner at last.

7

Family

There are ties that bind us to the people who really matter, sometimes through blood and sometimes through nurture. They create a powerful bond between parents, children and siblings that can enrich their relationship, despite any petty squabbles that are bound to arise over the years. Even when these ties seem weak or we believe they are broken, they remain somehow. I am beginning to realise that it has little to do with whether the relationship starts on a maternity wing, at an orphanage or in the freezer – kids, they mess you up... or is it, as has been said less delicately, the other way around? I wonder how long my children will have to spend in their little ice straws before they get really upset with me? In any other situation, deep freezing the kids and locking them away in a big chest for anything up to five years would be considered an extreme form of child abuse. I'm going to have to do some pretty fancy bridge building with the poor little mites one day. As and when they finally have the good fortune to be born.

Wednesday 30 May 2001

Lesley has remained stable now for the past three days. Not really any better, she is coping as well as she can. The doctors have told me all along that what we are doing here is managing the condition, not curing it.

'Critical OHSS requires multi-disciplinary management,' one of the doctors explained to me the other day.

In other words, they have to do lots of medical stuff to counter the symptoms of ovarian hyper-stimulation, and the best place to do that is somewhere with a high level of constant care, as found on the High Dependency Ward.

I'm starting to get the hang of this…

When I write off for my honorary medical degree as soon as all this is over, my specialist subject will be trying to decipher medical gobbledegook. This is probably enough to get you drummed out of the Royal College of Surgeons if you're caught. I imagine it's a bit like being a member of the Magic Circle. As soon as you start revealing how the tricks are actually done, they just don't want to know you any more.

I would not like anyone to confuse this cynicism for all things medical with any distrust of the wonderful doctors and nurses at Queen Charlotte's. On the contrary, I have nothing but love and admiration for all of them. And yes, I do mean *love*, in a real if surprising sense. It is as if they are family to me right now, they are very special. Their attention is unconditional, their efforts are unstinting and their dedication to pulling Lesley through all this is beyond question. What they are doing is protecting and caring for the most important person in my life and I couldn't be more grateful.

What a shame it is then, that an envelope popped through my door from our local private hospital this morning and put me in one of the darkest moods I have been in since this whole sorry saga began. Inside the envelope I found a bill for just over £600, covering the costs of the emergency treatment Lesley received there a week ago.

I am in shock. Have they any idea what physical and mental torture Lesley is going through? *Right now?* Can they even begin to imagine the emotional turmoil I have been going through since that terrible Wednesday?

On top of everything we are trying to cope with, this feels like a kick in the teeth. And, arriving at this still precarious stage of Lesley's recovery, it is just about as sensitive and logical a gesture as sending a kidnap victim's husband the bill for her food and lodgings, along with the expected ransom demand and one of her ears.

For now, I realise the best thing I can do is put aside my anger and drive to Queen Charlotte's. I have no intention of mentioning the bill to Lesley – she has more than enough to contend with at the moment. The nurses started her off with some physiotherapy on Tuesday afternoon, trying to get my wife to move her legs as much as she can to reduce the likelihood of a blood clot. This has been proving even more difficult than you would think, as such simple exercise feels like the Great North Run when you are operating on an eighth of your normal lung capacity.

Still, there are signs that Lesley's condition is easing a little, the chest drain is doing its stuff and I have a nice surprise for her today. Her sister Gwen travelled down to London last night with her two children, Laura and Daniel. I haven't told Lesley yet, but the plan is for me to meet Gwen between 2 and 3 o'clock on Du Cane Road, so that she can come in for this afternoon's visiting. If all goes well, they will all probably come by tomorrow, before heading home.

The last couple of days have already seen a number of other visitors come and go on the High Dependency Ward, so far without serious mishap.

Lesley has an aunt and uncle, Lynn and Nigel, who live in Chiswick, not that far from Queen Charlotte's. They are great friends to us, so were keen to call in on Monday and show their support. Lynn struggled visibly to contain her emotions when she saw Lesley propped up in her bed amid the tangle of tubes, and I thought Nigel's jaw was going to hit the floor. All the blood seemed to drain from his face, as he took in just how serious Lesley's condition was. Nigel doesn't really do medical situations and the hour or so he and Lynn spent at the hospital was difficult for both of them.

My brother David's wife Katharine has been working in London this week, so she also came by. Katharine is a very caring person and a great believer in alternative therapies. She is always full of advice about natural medicines, special preparations, aromatherapy and the like. Of course, the cynics among my family are never slow to voice their scepticism about all this stuff, but Katharine sticks to her guns. This time, though, even she had to concede that Lesley might need something a wee bit stronger than a bottle of Rescue Remedy to make her feel better.

Tuesday saw my brother Richard, his wife Liz and their young family arrive at Queen Charlotte's. The girls, Lauren and Amy, are very young and we had to handle things carefully, this is X-certificate stuff after all, but the visit went fine. When Lesley mentioned that we were supposed to be going to the theatre with Ellen this week, Richard's offer to book some tickets for us all to go to see the Abba show *Mamma Mia* in a couple of months' time brought a rare smile to my wife's face.

I am certain that this trickle through of familiar faces is helping keep Lesley sane through her current predicament. She needs something to connect her with her normal life, which otherwise feels so distant. And as hard as it may be to keep entertaining all these guests, it is something she can do to keep things together.

Leaving the hospital at 2 o'clock as usual today, I am excited by the prospect of meeting up with Gwen, as the visit of big sister from Manchester will mean so much to Lesley. I am getting used to the streets around here now, so I wander up to the local shops to await her arrival. By the time I meet up with her it is already getting on for 3 o'clock, so we walk briskly back to the entrance of Queen Charlotte's Hospital and I do my best to prepare Gwen for what will come next. As it happens, I do a woefully inadequate job.

When we walk into the High Dependency Ward, my wife is resting quietly and looks a picture of calm. The instant she sees her sister, Lesley's face goes from serenity to delight and then to panic, as she clutches her oxygen mask tightly to her face and takes several very deep breaths. She is so thrilled by Gwen's arrival that the excitement is proving to be a bit too much to cope with in her weakened state.

It takes her a full 10 minutes to regain her composure. When she does, Lesley teases Gwen, telling her sister that she has set her recovery schedule back at least a fortnight. I think Gwen realises she is only joking, but this is the first time she has seen Lesley this way and reality is biting.

The sisters talk for a while and find a way to share their strength, somehow pulling each other through the emotion of the moment. Then Gwen does something that no one else has thought to do in all the time Lesley has been in the hospital. She finds a hairbrush and brushes her sister's hair. For Lesley, this is just about the most fantastic thing anyone could do for her right now. Her hair has been a bedraggled mess since last Friday, when she collapsed wet through on her bed, following the abortive shower. Frankly, Lesley's hair has been the least of anyone's concerns over the past few days, but even this small amount of grooming helps her to feel human again. I wish I'd thought of it, but sisters know these things and Gwen obliges.

They continue to talk for some time, hampered only by the occasional need for Lesley to take a puff of oxygen through her mask. Without doubt, this is the happiest I have seen her for quite a while. It is not surprising that Lesley is disappointed when Gwen finally tells her it is time to go. The children are staying at her sister-in-law's and Gwen has to get back, but she will definitely come again tomorrow.

When I arrive home from the hospital, happy with the events of the day, Ellen has a surprise of her own. She has made a lemon meringue pie. It's very good and it reminds me of two things. One is that Lesley has never tasted one of Ellen's legendary lemon meringue pies. That's a point to me then. The other is that Lesley hasn't tasted *anything* for 13 days. 13 days! Most dedicated hunger strikers would have given up by now, or tried to chew their own arm off in some kind of ravenous fit. I find it impossible to understand and desperately hope that Lesley will be able to eat something soon. If it were not for those absurd levels of fluid retention, she would be wasting away before our eyes.

It is not until after Ellen has gone to bed that I dare take another look at the bill that arrived from our local private hospital this morning. It immediately provokes a range of unwelcome emotions and feelings deep inside me, but I read it a couple more times anyway and start to agonise over my response. I want to send back a long letter from some dark and angry place in my soul. I want to detail exactly what has been going on during the last few days. I want to tell them that it is all down to the fertility treatment they have already charged us a pretty penny for and that it is about time they took some responsibility for their actions...

In short, I want someone to blame.

And this little envelope full of cheer, minus even a suitably officious covering letter, has just put anyone and everyone working at the private hospital, where we have always felt so comfortable and well looked after, right in the firing line.

I am on page two of my letter before I am even close to calming down. Then I start thinking about Lesley's oldest brother, Barry. He has been calling her every day since he found out what has happened to his little sister. He is prepared to reserve judgement on whether the whole thing is really my fault, but Barry is in no doubt that someone ought to suffer for Lesley's misfortunes.

'Just say the word and I'll cave that consultant's head in,' he has offered more than once.

One piece of advice I would have for anyone even considering crossing anyone in Lesley's family is, 'leave it, it's not worth it'. This is real life *Eastenders* stuff we're talking about here, without all those namby-pamby Southerners running around the place. They have an expression for it in Lesley's hometown. *Radcliffe hard*.

Radcliffe is the kind of place where they eat kebabs off pizza bases and pub landlords think you are making it up if you try to explain that there really is such a thing as red wine. Above all though, it's an old Lancashire mill town, seven miles north of Manchester, and traditional values run deep.

Lesley's relatives don't always see eye-to-eye with each other, but take on any one of them and they close ranks quicker than you can say "family". Then they tend to hunt in packs and, believe me, they're big lads and formidable women, so you'd better watch yourself. Not that anything really unpleasant ever actually happens, as people back off pretty quickly when they see them coming.

I have already decided that I will not be handing over the IVF consultant at our local hospital to Barry. Our friends down on the fertility unit may not be my absolute favourite people right now, but deep down I know they are not to blame for what has happened. The reality is, fertility treatment does come with risks. Some of the risks may not be very well publicised, but publicised they are and they are very small. Lesley just happens to be on the wrong end of a normally reassuring statistic.

My letter to the hospital is still on the computer screen in front of me, the cursor blinking halfway down page two. I reread it carefully and digest my heart-felt expression of anger and frustration. *Three times*. Then I delete it. Every word. I replace the whole thing with just one sentence for our IVF consultant's attention.

'*I assume this has been sent to me in error.*'

I print my new letter out, fold it up with the bill and slide the whole lot into an envelope to post in the morning.

It is liberating to handle the situation in such a dispassionate way. My whole world has fallen into perspective in an instant and I know this is the last I will ever hear about the bill. Sometimes in life, administration becomes an end in itself and all you need to do is say 'no'. It's not personal, it's just another thing you have to deal with and move on. In a peculiar way, the correspondence that started my day as a real irritation has turned into something quite cathartic. It's late, but I have a feeling that I'm going to sleep better tonight than I have for some while.

Thursday 31 May 2001

Gwen knows exactly where to come today, so I meet her at the entrance to the High Dependency Ward. Laura and Daniel are with her and they are proudly carrying a plush toy. Kids can be remarkably impervious to harsh surroundings and Laura seems unfazed by the state of her auntie as she hands over the toy dog, a present that Lesley is delighted with. It is Daniel who notices that the unfortunate stuffed animal has immediately become smeared with blood from the pick-and-mix of gore-soaked tubes and dressings that serve as an ever-present reminder of Lesley's fortnight from hell.

I wince at the implications and difficult questions this might raise with the children, but Lesley brushes it aside with characteristic ease and a presence of mind she hardly seems entitled to in her current condition. She simply makes the practical suggestion that the dog should be called 'Mucky Pup'. This more than satisfies Laura and Daniel, who are both very happy with the name.

Yet another good idea I wish I'd thought of.

The leaving of Hammersmith is harder for Gwen today. She knows she won't be able to come back down right away, but promises to return soon. Her husband, Tony, is working shifts this week; hopefully he will be able to accompany the family on their next visit. Understandably, Lesley is emotional too, but she toughs out the moment and tells Gwen she won't be in the hospital for much longer anyway. She is determined to get herself out of here in days rather than weeks.

I try to nod encouragingly, but if the doctors are to be believed, this might be over-optimistic on my wife's part. The last woman they treated here for critical OHSS was in the hospital for more than six weeks. Her condition was nowhere near as serious as Lesley's has been, so I am learning to temper my expectations about when I might be able to get her home. Whenever it happens, I just want her to walk out of this place in one piece and never look back.

I'm pleased that Ellen is with me at Queen Charlotte's today. She helps to fill the void left by Gwen's departure and, once Lesley has recovered from the sad task of saying goodbye to her sister, there is another visible uplift in her mood. This is due almost entirely to these latest visits and Mucky Pup has now taken up guard at Lesley's bedside, a welcome reminder that everyone in both our families is rooting for her.

Despite another encouraging day, I am feeling anxious by the time Ellen and I arrive home tonight. There is only one thing I can think about. Tomorrow is Lesley's birthday. She will be 33 years old, stuck in a drab but functional hospital ward and dreaming about eating even so much as a dry biscuit, let alone a slice of birthday cake. Any plans for a fun weekend ahead, nights out on the town and such like, are long forgotten. So how can we hope to brighten Lesley's day, I wonder, and I can tell that Ellen is struggling with the same question.

Luckily for both of us, we are not the only ones working on the problem.

8

Happy Birthday

What's the very best thing you can do on your birthday? Be born, of course. Other interesting things might include sipping champagne on a beach in Bali as the sun fades on the horizon, or riding an elephant through a Sri Lankan jungle clearing. How about drinking dodgy red wine with 40 enthusiastic German tourists at 9 o'clock in the morning on a sailing ship off the coast of Croatia? Alternatively, you could visit wild orang-utans in the lush forests of Borneo, or you could eat strawberries dipped in chocolate washed down by a cool glass of Veuve Clicquot while cruising Scandinavia. Or maybe, just maybe, you could wake up in your own bed, away from the constant interruptions of a diligent medical staff. One day, my love, I promise, but not today.

Friday 1 June 2001

Most days before I set off for Queen Charlotte's Hospital, I work through a quick mental inventory of everything I need to take with me. Any personal items Lesley might need, cards from well-wishers, notebooks and pens, odd items of clothes. Whatever seems a good idea at the time, really.

Today this is an especially important part of my routine. Nothing can be left to chance. I have birthday cards from all over the country for Lesley this morning. I also have a present for her in the form of a battery-powered hand-held television to help while away some of the long hours. There are no such luxuries as your own personal television set on the High Dependency Ward, so I hope she will be allowed to use it.

I have even made a couple of A4-sized "birthday" posters to put up around her bed, featuring photographs of Lesley on top of the Empire State Building, looking and feeling great, if a little cold, smiling broadly at the camera. It has become hard to equate my wife with the woman who climbed all 354 steps to the head of the Statue of Liberty with me one Saturday morning little more than three months ago, during our pre-IVF treat – a long weekend in New York.

That was 11 March 2001, our first full day in the "city that never sleeps". The weather was bitterly cold, but we were up early and made it over to Liberty Island before 8 o'clock. It was quiet at that time of the morning, so the queue to climb the statue was very short. I couldn't help but suspect that the city does a bit of sleeping after all, but don't tell them I told you. Presented with this opportunity, we were brave enough (or foolhardy enough) to tramp up all those stairs to the big lady's crown. Once there, we had about 20 seconds to take in that famous view of the New York skyline before the flow of people swept us to the parallel stairwell to begin our walk back down again. Madness, but we wouldn't have missed it for the world.

The next ascent of our day was much easier, assisted as it was by the high-speed lifts of New York's impressive World Trade Center. We reached the 110th floor of the

South Tower in less than a minute, so I'm not sure if it was the sudden change in altitude or my general uneasiness with heights that made my legs wobble as I edged up to the floor-to-ceiling picture windows.

Among the usual gift shops, fast food restaurants and other tourist traps of this special observatory floor, we noticed an escalator and a line of people disappearing up it. Naturally, Lesley was keen to investigate. I was less enthusiastic. As we mounted the escalator, I jokingly suggested that it might be taking us all the way up to the roof. Lesley's stifled laugh was laced with the worrying suggestion that the joke might be on me, and I noticed that the knot in my gut was tightening in direct proportion to my height above sea level.

Sure enough, the escalator took us up to the roof. The roof of one of the tallest buildings the world has ever seen. Some 1,362 feet high – that's more than a quarter of a mile off the ground, out in the open air. But it was worse than that. Once you were up there, you had to walk almost a full lap around the roof before you reached the "down" escalator. My legs were swaying beneath me as we wandered slowly, and very carefully, around the top of the building. Even with my brain screaming 'too high!' at me, I had to admit the views across the city and of the now tiny Miss Liberty out in the bay were breathtaking. Lesley loved every minute of it.

I hope she will enjoy the posters, too. Not much, I know, but little reminders nonetheless of this happy weekend still so fresh in both our memories. New York City in early spring: a horse and carriage ride through Central Park; shopping at Bloomingdales; dinner on Times Square; and tickets for a Broadway show. Now that would have been a great way to celebrate a birthday.

As it is, we are here in the hospital and we will have to make do with the surroundings we have. The ward is hardly Party Central, but the nurses have brought Lesley a cake decorated with candles and sung "Happy Birthday" to her, even before Ellen and I arrived this morning. The cake was a wonderful surprise for Lesley. The fact that she can neither eat it, nor summon enough puff to blow out the candles, took nothing away from this thoughtful and touching gesture. The day has started well.

Within minutes of our arrival, Ellen and I have decorated the area around Lesley's bed, handed over her cards and presents, and my wife is busy opening them. I remind her that she will have three more visitors today. It's not that I'm expecting anything like the reaction we got from Gwen's surprise visit, but from now on I'm not taking any chances. Katharine will come again shortly, this time with my brother David, as they are both really keen to be here for Lesley's birthday. We are also expecting Claire, one of Lesley's closest pals, to come by sometime after lunch.

In the meantime, I am pleased to note that Lesley's progress this week has been impressive. Physically not a lot has changed, but she has an air of invincibility growing around her as her breathing continues to improve and she can now stand considerably longer periods off the oxygen mask. Lesley is still insisting that she will be out of here within the week and if there was one birthday present I could give her, that would be it.

There is a sense of fun on the High Dependency Ward today that I imagine is very rare indeed. Lesley is surrounded by all sorts of celebratory trappings that are violently at odds with the clinical nature of the room, but it is not until Katharine and David arrive that the party gets into full swing. In a move that could have been seriously misjudged but is actually pure genius, Katharine has brought with her a huge bag of party food. There are sausage rolls, cakes, little sandwiches, pork pies, mini sausages, soft drinks and an assortment of biscuits and crisps. A proper feast, and then some.

It's a fantastic idea, with only one slight drawback. The

birthday girl herself is in no position to eat any of these goodies, as much as she would love to. Lesley has still eaten nothing since the egg retrieval procedure, and any attempts to reintroduce the concept of food into her life have thus far been met either by a veto from the medical staff, or a stiff rejection letter from her stubbornly fragile constitution.

Not that this fact dampens Lesley's enthusiastic reaction to her sister-in-law's largesse – the party's the thing and it's another great example of family support just when we need it the most. Lesley is delighted by Katharine and David's wonderful gesture, so she invites everyone to tuck into the birthday picnic around her hospital bed. We all do, and the medical staff soon get in on the act.

It has been a pleasant enough morning, so during today's customary "quiet time" on the ward, Ellen and I take David and Katharine to a nearby pub. We all drink to Lesley's good health and her swift recovery.

As we walk back to Queen Charlotte's Hospital I feel good. For the first time in what seems like weeks, I notice that the sun is shining. This is my life now, I acknowledge with a shrug. I can barely remember anything different. Back and forth to Hammersmith each day has become a familiar habit. The route that seemed so strange to me at first is now etched into my own personal autopilot.

I've dumped work altogether this week, they can manage without me for now. And finding something to do with this middle hour has been a challenge at times, but I am getting to know the area well. Can I cope with four or five more weeks of this? Much more importantly, can Lesley? If we have to, yes, I am sure of it. We haven't come this far to let our resolve falter now.

Back on the ward, David and Katharine manage a last sausage roll and a cheesey straw, then say their goodbyes to my wife. I wave them off and await the arrival of Claire, who has phoned to say she is on her way.

Lesley calls me over and confesses that she has managed to eat one of the mini sausages. It was sitting there begging her to take a bite and she couldn't resist. What's fantastic about this is that Lesley has finally managed to eat something. What's not so fantastic is that the sausage was a bit spicier than she had expected and led to a pretty urgent call for a bedpan.

This last part is a little too much information for my liking, but it doesn't take away from the good news that she has managed to eat something and keep it down. It's Day 15 of her involuntary hunger strike and Lesley has at last taken a small step towards the light of a half-open fridge door. Despite the meagre scale of her achievement and the unco-operative reaction from my wife's stomach, I have to confess that this is the happiest a cocktail sausage has ever made me.

Claire's visit to the hospital brings me, and her as it turns out, back down to earth with a bump. As is my custom, I collect Lesley's friend from the hospital reception and try to prepare her for what she is about to see. By now I should be good at this, but I'm not. I'm rubbish.

I see Lesley every day and I know things have been even worse than they are now. Claire doesn't. Her only frame of reference for Lesley is from the real world, not this place. In the *real world*, Lesley doesn't have an oxygen mask, a chest drain, or any of that stuff. The Lesley that Claire knows is a dynamo, full of energy and fun. The last place she would expect to see her friend is in a hospital bed like this.

And apart from anything else, Claire hates hospitals. She is silent as she approaches Lesley's bed and my wife greets her with the biggest smile she can manage. One of the nurses is hovering nearby and asks if she can move some of the debris from our earlier picnic. Both Lesley and I turn to say 'yes', but when we look back in Claire's direction she has vanished.

The two of us exchange puzzled glances, then I walk around the bed to where Claire was standing. The first thing I notice is a soft panting noise and I find her sitting on the floor, arms folded tightly, and hyperventilating.

'It's OK,' she gasps. 'I'll be fine in a minute.'

This is the most extreme reaction yet; I'm just glad Claire didn't come here four or five days ago. At least Lesley is able to give her some reassuring signals, and her friend soon bounces back somewhere near to her normal self.

'I really hate hospitals,' Claire reminds me when she is ready to leave.

'Don't worry,' I tell her with a smile. 'Nobody noticed.'

Claire's visit has been another wonderful tonic for Lesley and a great way to wind up her birthday celebrations. I have made all sorts of rash promises today about where and how we might celebrate Lesley's next birthday, but if I'm honest I don't really care. As long as it is nowhere like this. All that matters for now is that we have made the best of this year's birthday and we can look forward to lots more. Lesley's not going to let this thing beat her. I know that for sure, because my dad told me.

9

Greens

When standing at the edge of a cliff, even shuffling backwards a couple of inches feels like progress to me. Truthfully though, it does very little to set my mind at rest. I can't bear to look down just yet, in case I am suddenly gripped with an irrational desire to leap forward and plummet onto the rocks below. I would never do that, of course. Just the fact that I could is enough. My eyes trace the cliff top trail off into the distance and I realise just how far I have come to get here...was the path really that narrow? And why did it never occur to me that there might be another route available? There are always choices in life, but I managed to blunder this way anyway. Looking ahead, the path definitely looks wider and I should be happy about that. The ground beneath my feet seems solid enough too, as I move away from the edge. But a bit of me still expects it to give way any second.

Saturday 2 June 2001
All the excitement of birthdays and managing Lesley's

social whirl of visitors over the past few days has taken my focus away from the real matter at hand: quizzing the doctors and extracting every last drop of information from them about Lesley's condition and, dare I say it, her recovery.

Following what can now only be described as the "spicy sausage incident", the doctors and nurses have gently introduced some real food into Lesley's regular routine. Small mouthfuls of meat, vegetables, pasta, potatoes and other such novelties now briefly interrupt the observations of Lesley's vital signs, the changing of various bags at the side of her bed and, of course, the once or twice daily conferences of all the available medical luminaries to discuss the best option or options for her ongoing treatment.

Today's topic is a familiar one. Do we go all-out to thin Lesley's blood, or is she in desperate need of a clotting agent to make sure we don't end up with an uncontrolled bleed? It sounds to me like you really shouldn't have both of these problems at the same time. But we do. Lesley, it appears, is very short of vitamin K in her blood and this, I am told, is probably the reason her blood is so thin. Well, that and all the Warfarin, everyone's favourite blood thinner and part-time rat poison. Lesley has had regular doses of the drug since arriving in hospital to reduce the risk of a fatal blood clot, which is danger *numero uno* in the OHSS game.

I need to understand more, so I get right in among the doctors standing around Lesley's bed as they discuss the possibility of giving her an injection of vitamin K, as this acts as the body's natural coagulant – it helps your blood to clot. Actually, I don't think they can quite make up their minds whether the vitamin deficiency has played a major part in thinning Lesley's blood, or whether her thin blood has caused the deficiency in vitamin K. I am waiting for someone to throw in a "chicken and egg" analogy, but these are serious chaps and the debate rages on for some time.

Whatever the truth is, I can only assume that vitamin K employs a pretty poor PR agency, as it rarely gets a mention in those Holland & Barrett adverts and, frankly, I've never heard of it. Even its name, K, suggests it's a long way down the vitamin pecking order.

The senior consultant at the middle of today's gathering is new to me, but he is obviously a blood specialist. Much of the discussion orbits his need to find out as much as possible about what is going on with Lesley. The new guy is openly frustrated by how thin her blood has become, and he seems to think that the team should do something about it urgently.

When he mentions the fact that certain foods, including some nuts and fruits, are known to stop the body's natural production of vitamin K, one of the other doctors suggests that this is probably not relevant given Lesley's recent diet.

'Aspirin can do the same thing,' the consultant points out.

Even I know that doctors sometimes prescribe half an aspirin a day to help "thin the blood". I'm guessing this goes to work on the vitamin K and helps to keep blood from clotting. But what do I know, and although I'm tempted to chip in my observation, I don't. The blood specialist is keen to confirm that aspirin has not been part of Lesley's treatment. Someone tells him it hasn't. Then he turns to me and asks for a stethoscope.

I am a little surprised by the request and can do nothing for a moment except stare at him blankly. Until it occurs to me what has just happened. Quite unintentionally, I have finally merged into the medical staff and been accepted as one of their own. I've been in their faces, persistent in my pursuit of information, and in the middle of every medical conference they've had about Lesley. Now it seems all I need is a stethoscope and I'll be ready for my new career in medicine.

The spell is broken as soon as one of the other doctors in the group hands over his stethoscope and the blood specialist gets on with a brief examination of Lesley. He still thinks a boost of vitamin K would help her system fight back from its perilous state, but they have to balance that benefit against the increased risk of a blood clot forming and the catastrophic effect this could still have on my wife.

It seems to me we have been down this road before. If we do one thing, we might endanger Lesley's life. If we don't, then the danger could be worse. It's the dilemma with Lesley's ever-present saline drip and the resulting fluid build-up all over again.

Following further discussion and much to-ing and fro-ing, the "blood clot" doctors concede the day, as the increased risk from this mild clotting agent is small. They bow to the specialist's experience and agree to give Lesley a vitamin K injection once a day for the next two or three days. Before he leaves, the specialist suggests that Lesley might also try to get the vitamins she needs through her food. Now that she has actually started eating again, anything seems possible.

Sunday 3 June 2001

Today is likely to be difficult. It's not that I have any fresh concerns about Lesley's rate of recovery. Apart from walking her vitamin K tightrope, she is ticking over nicely thank you very much, and all the other signs are good. No, the hard bit is going to come just after lunch.

When Ellen has to catch her train home.

Lesley's friend has been a rock. In a very hard place. I'm not sure how I would have coped with the last week or so without her around. And she has been a constant source of strength for Lesley when she needed her most. Saying goodbye later will be tough.

We arrive at the hospital this morning and walk into the

High Dependency Ward together. Ellen just wants to run in, give Lesley a big hug and apologise to her for having to leave. But first we endure a moment of alarm when we both register the fact that my wife is not in her bed. In my present state of mind, such a departure from the norm triggers the programming for sixteen shades of panic, and it takes me mere nanoseconds to paint a series of doom-laden scenarios for Lesley in my head.

Fortunately, nanoseconds are all I have, and I am relieved to see my wife walking slowly back round the corner, tubes and bags in tow, a broad smile on her face mocking my confusion.

'I thought that would surprise you,' Lesley whispers, concealing her breathlessness with a gentle chuckle, as she sits down rather awkwardly in the chair next to her bed.

'Well, you were right,' I confirm, shaking my head ruefully, but ruin the effect with one of my trademark *Wallace and Gromit* smiles.

It seems that when the nurses were trying to change Lesley's bedding earlier, she decided enough was enough. The usual procedure has been for them to roll her this way and that, as they ease the linen from under her and replace it. It's a routine that in her present state is uncomfortable, bordering on the excruciating. So this morning, Lesley convinced the nurses to let her visit the toilet while they got on with it.

Scaring the life out of me when I arrived on the ward was a calculated risk she was prepared to take!

It is not too long before Lesley clambers back into bed, but the break has done her good. So has practising her breathing all night. When Lesley struggled to get any sleep last night, she decided that focusing on her breathing for hours on end would be an excellent use of her time. And it has really made a difference. Lesley's confidence is growing to match her determination and I am actually daring to hope for the best.

While my brain is switched to "sensitive" mode, I decide to leave the two girls alone for a little chat while I visit the hospital shop downstairs and fetch up a couple of coffees. When I get back I deposit one of the drinks with Ellen and head off to find a doctor I can pester.

I can't praise the medical staff here highly enough, but there are a couple of doctors who have been around most of the time who seem to have made it their personal missions to pull Lesley through all this. So much has been going on that most of the team's names are a blur to me, but when I spot either of these two VIPs, I am reassured by their presence and delighted to have someone I can quiz mercilessly about my wife's progress.

The senior of the two is an experienced consultant gynaecologist and by far Lesley's favourite member of the medical staff around here. A handsome and dashing fellow in his early thirties, Stuart Lavery has a warm smile containing just the right amount of concern and total sincerity. He has impressed upon Lesley and me several times just how serious her situation has been. It has been his job to make many of the tricky decisions that have characterised my wife's treatment here or to ensure the chief consultant's decisions are carried out. Between Mr Magara's twice-daily visits to the ward, Stuart is an important man indeed.

The other almost ever-present doctor is tall, dark-haired and very, very busy. Striking both in looks and intelligence, Tara is still learning her trade and, I guess, is still in her twenties. Accurately fulfilling the "house doctor" stereotype, she appears to be on duty here for around 20 hours a day, in between writing up any notes and papers she needs for her studies.

I wonder what she does with all her spare time? She probably fills in on the maternity ward downstairs…

It is Tara I find today, and she updates me on the vitamin K saga. Having slept on it, the medical staff are a little more relaxed about the state of Lesley's blood today, although the vitamin K injection didn't happen yesterday as planned. Someone has clearly been given a rocket about this and Lesley has had her injection this morning.

The team on the ward are also doing their best to incorporate some greens into Lesley's food. One of the doctors here has a cub scout's badge in "healthy eating" or something. He has suggested that spinach is a good source of vitamin K. But it doesn't tend to turn up in the standard hospital fare too often, so Tara suggests that I bring some food with spinach in it for Lesley. She tells me that the nurses can heat it up in the ward's small kitchen area.

This sounds like a reasonable plan to me and I'm fairly sure spinach is one of those "super foods" we are all supposed to eat, full of vitamins and minerals that are very good for you. It's also one of those odd foods that come with an unusually large amount of baggage in the public consciousness.

What everyone knows about spinach, of course, is that cartoon hero Popeye loves the stuff. It has to be said though that *his* spinach does appear to be endowed with some kind of extra magical power. At the very least, it has a remarkable effect on his metabolism, as scoffing just a single can of it gives him enough strength to duff up anyone who happens to be getting on his nerves at the time. I know one or two people who can do the same thing after downing a couple of cans of Stella Artois, but that's a whole different set of chemical reactions.

Still, there's no getting away from it, he's quite a role model, that sailor man, and – despite any reservations you may have about his general behaviour – popular wisdom would suggest that he's right about spinach.

It all started with an eminent doctor and nutritionist who published a paper in 1870 claiming that spinach has no less than 10 times more iron in it than other similar green vegetables. Is it any wonder then that Popeye prefers spinach to steroids? Or at least he would if the doctor hadn't put his decimal point in the wrong place and gifted the Spinach Marketing Board a public relations boost that remains with us to this day.

I'm guessing that today's recommendation owes more to this little piece of nutritional mythology than any kind of grounding in scientific fact, but hey, it's worth a try. I decide to seek out some distinctly *spinachy* food for Lesley when I take Ellen to catch her train home at lunchtime. It is only when I check my watch that I realise how late it is. We will have to leave pretty soon.

When I return to the ward, the mood is sombre. Lesley and Ellen are quietly contemplating what comes next and I know that this is going to be the hardest leaving of all. We are all trying to be brave, but for each of us, things will change today. Big time.

For Lesley, it will mean that her only regular visitor will be me again. Tough break. She loses the chance to have all those special conversations only girls can have together. Especially in a situation like this.

For me, I am losing my housemate after what feels like at least 10 years. Has it really been only nine days since I picked Ellen up from the station? We owe her so much for being here, I really am so grateful.

As for Ellen, she is exchanging probably the most surreal "holiday" of her life for a return to work and a normal routine. It will be some adjustment to make.

'Hey Ellen, how was your week off?' I can hear her work colleagues asking her.

'*You really don't want to know.*'

Ellen is safely on board the Intercity train to Manchester Piccadilly as it glides away from Platform 6 at Watford Junction. I venture a final wave, but I'm not even sure she can see me through the reinforced train windows. I take a deep breath and turn towards the "Way Out Taxis" sign. *Is it just me, or does everyone who sees that sign expect to run into a spaced out hippy driving a Nissan Bluebird?*

As I head for my car, I'm feeling a bit light-headed. This morning has flown by and now, all of sudden, I am on my own again. We packed all of Ellen's stuff in my car before we set out for the hospital this morning, so we were ready to go. But everything seems to have happened in a rush. Even our goodbyes were muted, and tempered with disbelief that Ellen's visit could be over, with Lesley still stuck down at Hammersmith.

Before I drive back to the hospital, I remind myself that I have a job to do. The Harlequin Centre, Watford's gaudy but very popular shopping centre, looms large just a brief hop and a jump from the railway station. Surely the perfect place to lay my hands on some succulent spinach specialities?

A few minutes in and I realise my mistake. I would have been better off finding a local supermarket, as the mall is chock full with shoe shops, department stores and other icons of consumer paradise. It's a bit light on the spinach front. Fortunately, good old Marks & Spencer comes to my rescue, although even *their* food department is quite cunningly hidden and does take a bit of finding.

I trawl their shelves impatiently for anything that will offer up the magical greens that might provide a real boost of vitamin K for Lesley. They have lettuce – yes, plenty of that. Broccoli too. Even curly kale – weird looking stuff, I haven't seen it for years. All these jolly healthy leafy vegetables are probably just as good as what I'm looking for, and much more popular too, but I have my instructions. At last I hit the jackpot – spinach in its various forms! It takes me a few minutes to gather it up, but I finally emerge from the shop clutching a bag containing a chicken and spinach sandwich, a lamb and spinach *Karahi*, and a mini-pizza topped with spinach and mozzarella.

Oh, and a carton of milk. Not for Lesley, for me.

I always buy milk, it's a compulsion I have. Some people think it's strange, but one of these days, when they are there drinking a cup of black tea that could just do with a little splash of milk, it's me who will have the last laugh.

Back at the hospital, Lesley is noticeably quite grumpy, as she copes with life now that her friend has gone home. Her eyes have a harder, steely look that suggests I may have missed a few tears earlier and she is trying to be strong. I have a go at lightening her mood, but Lesley is not really playing and she simply assures me she is OK. When I tell her about my shopping expedition, she feigns interest.

'Did you buy any milk?' my wife asks straight away.

'No,' I lie. She knows me too well.

I explain the whole spinach thing. Super foods, vitamin K, Popeye the sailor man, the mistake with the decimal point. Lesley looks somewhat bemused as I produce the sandwich, the curry and the pizza from my M&S bag.

'And what am I supposed to do with all this?' she snorts, somehow offended by the arrival of these three ready-meals.

'Eat it, maybe?' I suggest. 'The nurses can heat it up for you and leafy greens are good for building up your vitamin K. Popeye would love all this stuff...'

'Popeye can keep his fucking spinach,' Lesley informs me. 'I'm not eating it. I hate spinach, it's horrible.'

I hadn't expected quite that reaction. For a moment I feel shocked and deflated after making a special effort to fetch the food all the way from Watford. It was pretty pricey too. And it is Marks & Spencer's, don't you know? Then, a little unexpectedly, I start to laugh. My mood dissolves immediately into an immense sense of relief and I can feel the beginnings of tears welling up in the corners of my eyes.

'*Popeye can keep his fucking spinach.*'

She's back! This is not the stoic survivor of the past

couple of weeks speaking now, as she battles through each day from one crisis to the next. This is the *real* Lesley I've been missing for too long. She is in control and suddenly I know for sure that everything's going to be OK.

10

Election day

Every time you knock on a door, there's no saying who or what might be on the other side. It could be a friendly face. It could be a big opportunity. Or it could be a madman with a chainsaw. Before the darn thing swings open you do your best to weigh up the hope and fear. Then you're in, and you have to deal with the consequences. But what happens if no one answers at all? You're tempted to push the door in yourself – open it up by whatever means possible. That can get you in a lot of trouble. I know that now. It really is a whole lot easier to go off and find another door. Even better, you could try being on the other side of the door in the first place. From there, you can open it with confidence whenever you like. And it feels great to walk out into the sunshine.

Tuesday 5 June 2001

Lesley's progress over the past couple of days has been fantastic. The physiotherapy has been getting a lot easier, she's kept up with her breathing exercises and – slowly but surely – some more of that excess fluid has been draining away. The poor girl is still carrying something like five stones of water in pockets around her body, but the pressure on her lungs and other vital organs is easing.

The biggest change, though, is inside Lesley's head. She can see an end to all this now and has no intention of staying in this hospital a minute longer than she has to.

'I'm going to be out of here by Election Day,' she tells me. 'I've never missed one before. I'm not going to start now.'

She is talking about the upcoming General Election, Tony Blair's opportunity to secure his place in history by retaining the keys to 10 Downing Street and winning a second term in government for his (new) Labour Party. The election is on Thursday. That's two – count them – two days away. Now I take no pleasure at all in playing the part of Mr Gloom and Doom, but this is ridiculous. Two days! We have no chance. How can I make Lesley understand?

'I have to go to the polling station on the day... because there's no way to organise a postal vote or a proxy... at this late stage,' she puffs, as I nod in agreement.

I so want to tell her she's lost the plot and that she needs to think of herself, not some silly election. Besides, we live in one of the safest Conservative seats in the country, so an extra vote either way is not going to make any difference.

But I can't say any of these things. Lesley really needs my support right now, so I try to make encouraging noises, without sounding too convincing. I'm hoping that something in her subconscious can read between the lines and get the message, or else we may have a crashing disappointment ahead of us on Election Day.

Not that crashing disappointments are anything new for us in these days of broken dreams and IVF hell. They have never been far away where elections are involved either. Lesley and I first met on a street corner in the run up to the General Election in June 1987. Meeting Lesley, I hasten to add, was no disappointment at all. Not for me anyway. And it was all her mum's doing, she set us up.

Lesley's mum was busy running the Radcliffe Labour Party's base of election operations from the family home that fateful day, when I appeared to volunteer my services for canvassing duty. She must have liked what she saw, as she swiftly dispatched me off to a street where I found Lesley and her dad knocking on doors and ticking supporters off an unfeasibly long list.

The object of calling at everyone's door during elections, by the way, is not, as some mistakenly believe, to convince people to vote for your candidate. Not a bit of it. All a political canvasser ever wants to do is find out if you are going to vote their way or not, and then get on to the next door as fast as possible. This simple piece of information means that, come Election Day, the activists know exactly who to call for and offer a ride to the polling station, and which doors to superglue shut until after the polls close.

The disappointment around the 1987 election was the usual one. Labour didn't win. Again. But Lesley and I formed a coalition of our own and we were married just over a year later. So at least we had some compensation for what turned out to be another four years of Margaret Thatcher. *Somehow the NHS survived, so I guess I have something else to be grateful for.*

When I talk to the doctors at Queen Charlotte's today I am fishing for good news, but I am also looking for some rational arguments that might temper Lesley's expectations of an early escape. As it happens, there's a decent helping of the former and very little to dampen my wife's enthusiasm. It is so long since I have felt that things were really running our way that I find it hard to comprehend at first.

They tell me they are going to remove Lesley's chest drain this morning. And they are making arrangements to move her from the High Dependency Ward to a regular ward later. This is big stuff, and I feel a little nervous when

I finally get my head around the implications. We're talking about a major scaling down of Lesley's treatment regime here. She is eating and drinking small but regular quantities now, so the saline drip is a thing of the past. And it has just registered with me that the tube is missing from her nose. Her catheter was removed yesterday too, and she has barely needed a boost of oxygen from her handy bedside mask all morning.

It's all good news.

I am almost ready to join Lesley's escape committee when I imagine Steve McQueen getting caught up in that fence in *The Great Escape*. So close, but we need to be wary of any last minute hitches.

The removal of Lesley's chest drain is over in moments and, despite leaving an unpleasant open wound, the relief on her face is great to see. Lesley is even more convinced she can get out of here by Thursday and, as I watch her eat a light lunch, I am starting to buy into the dream.

I make myself scarce as usual at 2 o'clock and the nurses suggest I give them a couple of hours today. When I return, I expect Lesley to have moved. The regular ward is only a matter of a few strides down the corridor, but to us it feels like a million miles. Eight beds instead of two, a drastically reduced nurse to patient ratio and a peculiar sense of homeliness when set against the austere spaciousness of the finest High Dependency ward the NHS has to offer.

As I enter this new ward for the first time, I am struck by how different it feels to be visiting Lesley this afternoon. I see many of the same faces among the medical staff, though they are spread thinner here. There are seven other patients too, all with their own problems. Some are sleeping and some have visitors, but they all look thoroughly miserable.

I wonder how I look to them?

It's a bit of a shock to see so many people dotted around

the room compared to what we're used to, and it's obvious I'm going to have to learn to behave myself in here – something I'm not that used to. But for all that, it's normal. This is what I expect a hospital to be like and, with the limited experience I have of such places, it feels like we are a little nearer the exit. Just over a week ago that would not have been a nice feeling at all. Now it comes with a welcome sense of reassurance.

Thursday 7 June 2001

It's Election Day. I wake up this morning with those butterflies in my stomach that have been with me on the day of every General Election for as long as I can remember. That's 27 years I realise, give or take.

I was just nine years old when I first stood for Parliament. We organised a mock election in our class at my junior school to coincide with 1974's second General Election in October. That's the one where Harold Wilson scraped home with a majority of three – just enough seats to muddle through, after not quite making it the first time round in February.

Three of us put ourselves forward as candidates for the main parties and we all had to address the class before the vote. To say I was confident as we headed for the "hustings" would have been a lie, as early straw polls around the class suggested that I would be lucky to pick up even a couple or three votes in the Tory heartland of Connaught Road Juniors.

My Conservative rival was hot favourite to win and he spoke first, making empty promises about sweets all round in a remarkable effort to foreshadow the sleazy downfall of his party's government more than two decades later.

The Liberal was up next and he didn't seem at all sure what he was promising, but he was a jolly nice bloke.

Me, I was proper "old Labour" even at that tender age and I outlined a programme that covered all the issues that keep nine-year-olds awake at night – inflation, the balance of payments crisis, the NHS and unemployment. The other kids stared open-mouthed as I rattled off my political agenda, based firmly on the Labour Party's 1974 election manifesto.

Amazingly, I won with 25 out of 33 votes, Labour's biggest landslide victory of the last century by my reckoning.

So the whole "butterflies on Election Day" thing has been fluttering around my psyche for a very long time. But the feeling in my stomach this morning has nothing to do with the General Election or any such nonsense – I have much bigger things to get worked up about right now.

Lesley is coming home today.

I pinch my arm a couple of times, even before I drag myself out of bed. Just in case I'm only dreaming. Lesley *may* be coming home today, I correct myself. I need to remember that nothing is certain yet. The exit polls are in and the doctors say she will probably be allowed to come home this afternoon, but the final votes are still being counted. This is not a time for overconfidence. We've come too far to get carried away now. And if I've learned anything about days like this over the years, it's that they don't always end the way you think.

I need to call the hospital to make sure things are still on track. The doctors held another one of their impromptu "around-the-bed" conferences last night. It was more like a hostage negotiation than a medical discussion, but the team finally agreed to Lesley's demands. They were pretty keen for her to stay in the hospital for a few more days under continuing observation. But if she had a good night, and if the chief consultant gave his blessing, they reckoned that Lesley could come home today.

I still can't believe it when the nurse on the ward tells me that Lesley has indeed had a good night. That's one big tick in the box – we will need two more before the end of the day for Lesley to be happy. One will be on Mr Margara's discharge sheet and the other on a ballot paper.

Driving down to Hammersmith, I start thinking how much I will miss this journey down the M1 and round the North Circular every day. It will be forever right up there on that list of things I'd really rather be doing than living a normal life. Somewhere just below contracting bubonic plague and having my legs gnawed off by an angry badger.

When I reach Du Cane Road, parking is a familiar problem. It doesn't matter to me, as I know where I want to leave my car today, once more for old time's sake. I pull in opposite the prison gates of Wormwood Scrubs and look over at the nearby parking ticket machine, which is…

Working?

I can't believe they've gone and fixed it. What kind of start to my day is that? I have my little notice ready to display on the car dashboard and everything. Thwarted, I fumble for some change and buy a parking ticket. I have no choice but to put several hours on it, as I have no idea how long I will be here today. Absurdly, I can't help feeling cheated as I walk down to the hospital, but I manage to convince myself that the ticket machine's recovery is somehow linked to Lesley's. Perhaps my money-munching pal represents a positive start to the day after all.

Everything seems very normal at Queen Charlotte's when I arrive. I'm expecting a ticker tape parade and marching bands, but there is no indication of the momentous events to come. Some sort of oversight I presume, although it is possible I am letting my expectations run away with me a little.

Lesley is in good spirits on the eve of her greatest triumph. No one thought she would be in shape to get out of here today. Especially not me. So, as we await the nod from Mr Margara, it is hard not to get too excited and noisy, thereby upsetting all the other patients on the ward. I make my apologies, then I comment on the fact that

Lesley has shed quite a few pounds of excess fluid, even since last night. That's without the assistance of the effective if unspeakable chest drain.

'Yes, I'm peeing loads,' she murmurs, absent-mindedly. The niceties of modern conversation are not really part of Lesley's current reality. She's just happy to be allowed to go to the toilet on her own, without any trailing bags or tubes to worry about or trip over.

It is just after one of these regular toilet breaks that the seemingly ever-present Tara comes by to check up on Lesley. I hadn't realised, but she is writing up a paper on my wife's treatment. In her copious spare time. Lesley's condition really has been the worst case of ovarian hyper-stimulation syndrome any of the doctors or nurses here has ever seen, so it seems fitting that someone should write it all up.

And Tara is not the only one. Two of the student nurses have used their experiences of looking after my wife in case studies on "critical care" for their own qualifications. Only yesterday, one of them was thrilled to inform Lesley that her case study had just helped her to get her diploma.

You might think that my wife would find all this attention rather intrusive, especially after all she's been through lately. But she is made of sterner stuff. Lesley tells me that she is delighted some good may come from her stay in hospital and, more importantly, that it may help others who come after her. It's a real "Tiny Tim" moment and I have to stifle a tear.

When the boss man finally appears, both clock hands are touching midday. He is brusque and busy, the consummate professional and, as ever, possesses the subtlety of a steamroller. But I see something else in Mr Margara's eyes today. There is a little sparkle that tells me two things. He is immensely proud of his team who have ventured into our personal hell and dragged us back out. There's also an unspoken admiration for Lesley, who has done so much to heal herself and come out of this fighting, when the easy thing would have been to lie down and wallow in the misery of it all.

He tells Lesley she can go home with what looks suspiciously like the corners of a smile and signs her discharge form. We both thank him for everything, but he's gone before we can catch our breath. Mr Margara has other speeding bullets to catch, other tall buildings to leap in a single bound. All that remains is for us to pack up and go.

It's a deliberate process. We need to gather all of Lesley's things – her clothes, her drugs, her cards and papers. That's the easy bit. Finding something reasonable for Lesley to wear is harder. She is still around three or four stones heavier than normal and that won't change until, as my wife so delicately puts it, she 'pees it all away'. Which is not going to happen in the next half hour or so. In short, Lesley's clothes are not exactly made to measure right now, so we end up with a fetching combo of nightwear, underwear and loose fitting normal stuff. It will have to do.

Before we leave, I run around the place thanking as many doctors and nurses as I can. I am alarmed when I realise that there is no sign of either Stuart or Tara. We can't leave until they have had their curtain call.

Suddenly I spot Tara, walking off down a corridor. I give chase and intercept her on a staircase. She looks a little surprised as I shake her hand and thank her. She thanks me too and tells me that she's learnt a lot from having my wife here. When I get back to the ward, Stuart has found Lesley.

'You have to understand how serious all this has been,' he tells her, probably for the fifth time. 'You've been very lucky. A lot of people wouldn't have got through it.'

Lesley nods and wipes her eyes. It is amazing that there are still some tears left after everything that has happened. Stuart stands up to leave and I shake his hand too.

'*Never* put yourself in that position again,' he warns, as he walks away. '*Never, ever*'.

Lesley and I just look at each other. We don't need to say anything. Instead we gather the last few bits of her stuff and walk slowly towards the lift. Downstairs, I suggest Lesley waits in reception while I retrieve the car from Wormwood Scrubs. She has a better idea. There's no way Lesley is swapping her incarceration here for a visit to the prison gates, but she can't wait to step outside and smell the fresh air.

For me, walking out of the hospital with Lesley on my arm is like the release of Nelson Mandela, the fall of the Berlin Wall and that bit where Tim Robbins squeezes through the tunnel he's been digging for 19 years in *The Shawshank Redemption*. All rolled into one. It was dark when we arrived here just over two weeks ago. Right now the sun is shining. The metaphors are almost overwhelming.

Leaving my wife safely perched on a convenient wall in front of the building I find myself almost running along the road to my car. Minutes later we are on our way home. Lesley remains adamant that we still have to make time to vote today. It's important. Universal suffrage is a hard earned right – it's not to be taken lightly. The whole idea of getting out to vote on Election Day has given her that final impetus to get well and get home. And Lesley has done more than enough *suffraging* lately to not get her wish.

After a suitable settling in period at home, we pop down to the polling station, just two minutes away by car. We see one of our neighbours is helping out on the desk where they hand out the ballot papers. Her eyes are out on stalks when she spots the super-sized Lesley shuffling in to vote. I am reminded that we have a long recovery ahead of us before everything can possibly return to normal. That's if we can even remember what *normal* is any more.

Lesley scrawls an X on the ballot paper and is delighted

to fall into her own bed when we get home. She needs to get some proper rest ahead of a long evening in front of the General Election news coverage, looking out for our local result and keeping our eyes peeled for what's happening in Radcliffe. I had almost forgotten that my own brother, Alan, is standing for Labour in the safe Conservative seat of Worthing too. He doesn't stand a chance of course, but like Lesley, he is giving it his best shot.

When our local result comes through in the early hours of the morning, the Tories have notched up a paltry 23,230 votes in our constituency and they have a majority of just over 10,000. Lesley is far from disappointed. The Labour candidate came third with an impressive total vote of 11,338. Without Lesley's support, he'd have only had 11,337. And that really wouldn't have been good enough.

With this news, we prepare to sleep and, for the first time in a while, my thoughts drift back to Harley Street and our six frozen embryos. *That was what all this was about, wasn't it?* And the embryos are still there, locked up tight in their sub-zero vault, just waiting for us to say the word. Lesley and I have talked about them a couple of times, but it has been so hard to imagine our lives beyond the critical care environment that these conversations have simply dried up.

No matter, we will have plenty of time to make decisions and plan our next steps later. When Lesley is fully recovered, feeling fit and has come to terms with everything the OHSS has thrown at her. Although I doubt that will be any time soon.

11

Wandering

Somewhere in my extensive book collection is a tatty old paperback called "Mind Swap" by Robert Sheckley. It's a tragic-comic tale about a guy who finds himself travelling the universe, desperately searching for something. He hops from planet to planet aboard ramshackle spaceships and jumps through interplanetary portals, all without success. Finally, he hits upon a plan. He simply stops where he is and puts his feet up. The theory being that, sooner or later, everything in the universe will wander by and, inevitably, what he is looking for will come to him. It seemed far-fetched when I read it the first time, but I'm beginning to wonder. I'm the one looking for something now – perhaps it's time for a new plan, perhaps it's time to stop and wait for that something to find me.

Wednesday 26 September 2001

Life can be hard. Here we are, sitting by the pool at our hotel in Limassol, Cyprus. Late season, beautiful weather – it's just right for a quiet relaxing break. We certainly need it, but there's something wrong with this picture and things haven't been quite right for several months now.

Our lives have stalled. We're frozen here in what feels like an ever-expanding moment of time that began three months ago and shows no signs of letting up. Neither Lesley nor I have any real idea how to get things moving again, or even how to put it into words. We talk, but never about *that* subject. The events that have taken over our lives have somehow been locked up in the "too difficult" box and we are both terrified to open it.

I was full of optimism back in June, when Lesley came out of hospital, but I should have realised that the scars left by the ovarian hyper-stimulation would be more than skin deep. Even a trained chimp could have guessed that Lesley would take some time to make a full recovery, but the euphoria of the moment was irresistible to me.

I definitely should have read the warning signs when the hot water pump for our central heating broke the day after I brought my wife home from Queen Charlotte's. There they were, all the hallmarks of another clumsy metaphor – the mystical significance of which was just crying out to be interpreted – and all I could think about was the lack of hot water in the house.

It's a good thing we have such brilliant neighbours – Joan and Ken on one side, Estelle and Tom on the other – they had all offered to look out for Lesley when I was at work, and to bring her some lunch each day while my wife was still laid up in bed, finding it hard to get about the house. Unfortunately, none of them are experts when it comes to fixing central heating systems, but I know a man who is. My mate Trevor from across the road has saved our bacon on more occasions than I care to count. He's a top-notch boiler man and self-confessed *bodger par excellence*. Armed with what looked to me like a couple of bottle tops and a shoelace, Trevor fixed the pump for us in no time. He wouldn't even take any money from me for his trouble.

'Tell Lesley, that's a bunch of flowers from me,' he winked, finishing off a cuppa and a customarily good-humoured chat.

There's something of the cockney wideboy about our Trev and he revels in the fact that he fitted and maintains a boiler for TV's "Del Boy" Trotter, David Jason, who lives just a few miles up the road. He also credits Lesley and me with having brought a bit of excitement to the otherwise dull cul-de-sac we all live on. To the uninitiated, it might seem that Trevor is as mad as a box of frogs, with his unique and delightfully eccentric take on life. Me, I wouldn't swap him for the world and you'd have to go a long way to find a truer, more reliable pal.

The days that followed Lesley's return home crawled by, uncomfortably in the most part for her, both physically and emotionally. Lesley spent a large proportion of the time in bed, convalescing, as her body grew stronger and all that troublesome fluid drained away.

A couple of weeks in and my wife found herself at our local doctor's surgery. Lesley explained what she'd been through but, despite her almost superhuman recovery rate, it was upsetting to admit that she still felt rubbish. As amazing as it may seem, the "effective care following extreme trauma in the form of critical OHSS" didn't appear on any of the dropdown menus on our GP's computer screen, so he thought about it for a while and simply prescribed Lesley another fortnight at home. *With plenty of fluids and plenty of rest.*

That simple phrase still chills me to the bone, and it was hard not to feel disheartened at the lack of solid advice or practical help available to us. *Anywhere.*

Forced to work out her own therapy, Lesley seized the opportunity to catch the whole of Wimbledon fortnight before going back to work – that was the one positive she could grab with both hands, after an otherwise unproductive session at the doctors'. As a tennis fan, the chance to relax in front of the television and take in one of the sport's premier competitions from start to finish cheered Lesley up no end.

By the time Goran Ivanisevic had hit his final shot in anger and walked off with the Wimbledon Men's Championship, the signs were there that my wife was ready for her own Centre Court and a dramatic return to work.

Lesley's life was visibly slipping back into its normal groove. She now weighed in at around nine stones lighter than when the OHSS fluid build-up was at its peak. She was fully mobile and was getting around easily without any undue breathlessness or tiredness. To everyone else, Lesley's recovery was right on track and, considering the scare we'd had, things had worked out fine.

Despite everything, we had managed to bank six embryos down at the embryology clinic in London. They were "safe", as any dodgy Sunday afternoon television gameshow host might say, just before tempting you to gamble everything for the chance to win a caravan or, if you are really lucky, a speedboat. All being well, sometime soon we would be ready to spin that IVF wheel of fortune again, with no significant risks to Lesley's health this time. The process would involve three main steps and none of them promised either a speedboat or any of the difficulties and dangers that came with producing the eggs in the first place.

First, we would have to thaw out some embryos – the biggest risk being that they may not survive the process. Next we would "down-regulate" Lesley's hormonal cycle using a "sniffer", which as the name suggests is a mild drug concoction inhaled nasally (don't ask me why, but it works). Then, at the right moment, the embryos would be popped into Lesley's womb.

Put this way it all sounds so simple. I can only guess at the turmoil in Lesley's head, every time she has even contemplated any of this after her recent trauma.

The problem, if only we could have identified it in those first few weeks, was that we had both had a real and unexpected shock and everything we thought we knew about our lives had been turned upside down. If you had asked Lesley back in April what she would have done to have a child, the answer would most probably have been 'just about anything'. Suddenly, this could no longer be true. Suddenly, our ten-year obsession had become a lot less important. Suddenly, I found myself contemplating the alternatives.

Could we just put a stop to this thing altogether? What did we need kids in our life for anyway? But if we did... what else could we do? That little voice inside my head was back again I realised, whispering softly. Something about the "A" word. Something about drawing a line under everything and trying something new. I wasn't sure what I really wanted to do, and I certainly couldn't think of any way to broach the subject with Lesley. So like a proper man when faced with any kind of emotional turmoil, I bottled it up and got on with other things instead.

Just before she returned to work, Lesley had a scheduled appointment with Mr Margara down at Hammersmith. At the main hospital this time, where he held his regular fertility clinic. The meeting was part check-up and part to explore the possibility of continuing Lesley's treatment under his care.

It wasn't that the team at our local private hospital couldn't be trusted with our last hope of parenthood. Not at all. But we were pretty messed up at this point and "mixed emotions" barely covered how we were feeling. Underlying everything was the notion – right or wrong – that whatever had happened at the fertility unit down the road had ended badly a few weeks before. While at Hammersmith they had pulled several rabbits out of the hat and somehow Lesley had come through it all in one piece.

Nobody at our local hospital was to blame for what happened. Nobody. We knew that then and we know it now – it just happened. The only thing we could hope to control was what might happen next. And if any of that *happening* was ever going to be down at the little fertility unit that had always felt so cosy and safe…well, we both knew we weren't ready for that just yet.

So we asked Mr Margara if he would take us on as patients, if and when we decided to proceed with further treatment and make use of our frozen embryos, still shivering somewhere in their liquid nitrogen overcoats.

'Just look at this woman!' the consultant beamed, as we entered his office. 'She is looking much better now than when she was here last time, don't you think?'

Mr Margara happily agreed to take us on as patients when the time was right, and what really struck me that day was the genuine warmth of his welcome and the transparent pride he took in Lesley's progress. This was a side of the man that had never been quite so obvious back on the ward four weeks earlier, when he had been busy with the task of saving my wife's life.

So once again we walked out of Queen Charlotte's Hospital, the sun shining brightly and looking to the future. This time we were armed with a bunch of new pamphlets, the support of a fine specialist we owed so much to, and the first inkling of a plan. But absolutely no idea of a timetable for what we should do next or any way of dealing with the emotions of the moment.

The fact that we'd even managed to ask about future treatment at Hammersmith was encouraging, but I think we were just going through the motions. In reality, we were still finding it almost impossible to connect up the dots to our life before OHSS and even harder to plot our next steps.

It was fast becoming obvious to me then that even with four highly competent and professional medical establishments in our orbit, none of them could really offer anything to help us get through the next few months. At Queen Charlotte's, they had done what they could, at least for the time being, while the clinic in Harley Street was no more than an embryo storage facility for us now. The team at our local fertility unit could only help us if we decided to go back there to continue our treatment. And our GP was willing, but he was incredibly detached from all of our problems by now. We had no obvious place to turn.

So we planned holidays instead. We needed something to look forward to and we were only too aware that we hadn't had much in the way of a proper holiday for a few years. Our recent weekend in New York and a winter break in Cyprus a couple of years back being the main exceptions. It may not be in any textbook, but we decided right then to see if we could do without counselling or other more practical support by simply travelling the world.

'Can we afford it?' we wondered.

Of course not – we'd spent all our money on fertility treatment of one kind or another over the past five years and the cupboard was bare.

'Do we care?' was our next thought.

No – we were alive and that was what really counted. And who knows, maybe we would hit upon some kind of revelation on the way? Perhaps that little voice in my head might even come up with something useful for a change? Some pearl of wisdom that would make sense of everything and guide us on our way. If not, we could have fun looking for it and hang the expense.

Before we could change our minds, Lesley had booked us on a guided bus tour of the USA's West Coast: a late December flight into LA; New Year in San Diego; then on to Las Vegas and San Francisco. That ought to blow the cobwebs away, although the trip is already provoking mixed emotions, given what happened a couple of weeks ago. The

9/11 attack on New York's World Trade Center shook the world and we certainly felt it keenly enough, despite (or perhaps because of) our other preoccupations.

I vividly recall that queasy moment I had, standing on the roof of the building's South Tower exactly six months before the shocking events. It has put a whole different slant on our problems, but on balance, we are still very much looking forward to our American adventure – if only to share in a spirit of defiance we already feel well bought into.

But we won't be going until the end of the year and that is just too far away. So we grabbed a last minute "cheapie" to Cyprus a few days ago and jumped on a plane.

And it really is lovely here in Limassol, if a little down market from the beautiful town of Paphos we visited last time we were here. I have to admit it is a bit "Brits-abroad" around town, but it's late in the season and is remarkably quiet. Most of the pubs, clubs and restaurants have been wound down, but as many of them have pictures of bulldogs outside and are decorated with Union Jacks or offers of "full English breakfasts", I suspect this is no great loss.

There's not much to do apart from relax. And talk. So, sitting by the pool in Cyprus, we talk. About booking another holiday. We fancy the Far East after the USA. It's somewhere we've never been, with a whole new set of cultures to experience and an almost infinite capacity to take our minds off the obvious. I am beginning to think we will never touch on the subject of our embryos and everything that comes with them ever again. Then, out of the blue, Lesley simply opens up.

'I'm scared,' she whispers.

'Of more treatment?' I prompt.

'Not really. It's you…'

'*Me?*' I scream silently, but I keep my mouth firmly shut. '*What could I have possibly done?*' Despite my alarm, I reach out a reassuring arm and suggest we pop inside for a coffee.

'I'm scared that you can't bear to wait for me – that you will push me into it. Can you understand that?' Lesley asks me, her voice cracking over a steaming hot caffè latte.

Actually, I can't understand it at all and my brain is still screaming at me in protest. But I'm a good listener, so I say nothing and let Lesley continue.

'This whole thing, you know…well, it's done my head in. The thought of going back for more treatment – even if they say it's safe – it just freaks me out. And I know you want me to, but I can't. Not yet anyway…'

She pauses to catch her breath.

'Maybe never…I just don't know. And I wouldn't blame you if you can't wait for me…'

As Lesley's voice trails off, we are both trying our best to choke back the tears. I am horrified to think that she has been bottling all this up for the last 10 weeks. I know Lesley has been struggling to come to terms with the blows she's taken lately. So have I. God knows, we have both been on the edge of post-traumatic stress at times.

Problems with concentrating and sleeping? Check.

Feelings of isolation and detachment from life? Check.

These are classic tell-tale signs, and who could say they are unexpected?

But this? '*I wouldn't blame you if you can't wait for me. I'm scared that you will push me into it.*'

How can she think that?

'I would never, ever, ever…do that,' I stutter. 'I would never force you to do something you didn't want to do.'

'I'm scared that you would,' she sobs.

I don't know what to say. I really wouldn't push Lesley into anything like this. *Never, ever.* I'm not lying.

When I was lucky enough to get my wife back on Election Day in June, the whole idea of continuing with the treatment was the last thing on my mind. Even now, any real enthusiasm for doing so is probably coming from some kind of misplaced loyalty to our frozen embryos. Those poor little specks of life are the forgotten victims in all this, although my guess is that right now they don't really give a hoot.

I try my best to comfort Lesley and assure her that she has nothing to fear. How has she got it into her head that I am so enthusiastic about having children anyway? So enthusiastic that I would be willing to gamble with her life? Just the thought of it makes my blood run cold.

Nothing could be further from the truth. If I'm completely honest – and I realise that now is not exactly the right time for such candour – having kids of our own has never been that big a deal for me. Important, yes, but it has never seemed entirely real. Even at 36 years old, I can be like a kid myself sometimes. And I quite like that.

Of course, I've always gone along with that sitcom ideal of forming a perfect family unit, even if my hopes and dreams are more Homer Simpson than John-Boy Walton. And I've happily coped with all the fuss and the heartache that comes with IVF. But given the choice, having my wife here fit and well means much more to me, and it always will. If I'm honest, I think I'd rather call a halt to any potential treatment right now and go off and discuss the benefits of childlessness with that little voice in my head. It just feels like we have unfinished business.

Naturally I skip some of these details, in case Lesley gets the wrong idea all over again, but we sit and talk for hours. That's at least a couple of months' worth of proper talk, all in one afternoon. We need it desperately.

All those thoughts, all those fears – they are finally out in the open where they belong. Released from the pressure we've been under, even if only for today, there is a palpable sense of relief in the air as we head back outside. At last, all the second-guessing and walking on eggshells, all the unrelenting sadness of the past few weeks can be put to one side and, finally, we manage to laugh. Together.

We are remembering our first trip to Cyprus, only a couple of years ago. We had a wonderful day exploring

Paphos – the quaint town centre, a picturesque fort at the harbour, the old-fashioned streets and a nice restaurant for lunch – taking photographs wherever we went. It was only when we returned to our hotel in the late afternoon that we realised we had no film in our camera. Every shot we had carefully framed, posed for or simply snapped was entirely in our imagination.

Isn't it amazing how getting one simple thing wrong can mess up all your plans?

Refusing to accept defeat, we loaded the camera and headed out the very next day to recreate our holiday album. Racing round in half the time, we occupied our own special world of *déjà vu*, quickly taking every shot all over again, and this daft experience became one of the most treasured memories of our week away.

It feels great to be able to laugh about it now, but before we head for the USA at the end of December I'm going to buy a digital camera...

Monday 1 June 2002

I close my eyes, take a deep breath and savour the balmy sea air. This is one of those days I promised Lesley...

Can it really be a whole year ago?

We are eating a celebratory dinner on a chequered patio next to the beach and there's a man here, playing the guitar. Not particularly well, but he's giving it a good go, while two others are singing an Indonesian/English hybrid version of "Happy Birthday" to my beautiful wife, who is resplendent tonight in her finest evening gown. We chink our champagne glasses against the moonlight and toast the occasion.

The beach here is amazing, lit up as it is by strategically positioned flaming torches, and it doesn't matter how you cut it, the Nusa Dua Resort in Bali is a bit of an upgrade on Lesley's accommodation this time last year.

We are in the middle of our much-anticipated Far East

tour, having already breezed through Bangkok and Singapore on the way here. We'll be off again soon to Hong Kong, before we take the long flight home, but for now it's time to sit back and relax in one of the most beautiful places on earth.

This trip is the culmination of all our travel plans, all our extravagant attempts to avoid the elephant in the room and get on with something far more interesting instead. Just because our elephant is more like a woolly mammoth in the freezer matters not a jot. Lesley and I can ignore it just the same. We've had months of practice.

Not much has changed since our heart-to-heart in Cyprus last year. It felt like a major breakthrough at the time and I suppose it was. We were in a dark place back then, probably much darker than I had ever imagined, and it was a small step towards the light. But we have a long way to go before everything that 2001 kindly threw at us can be consigned properly to the past.

I am beginning to realise that Lesley will need quite a few more birthdays like this one before we are ready to move on with any plans. Before we can even think about thawing out those little "popsicles" still waiting for us in Harley Street.

12

Decisions

The clock is ticking, counting down your life. If you're lucky you might have 27,000 days to play with. Give or take quite a few, based on variables such as regular exercise, a healthy diet, genetic abnormalities and not being run down by a bus. That's a generous enough allowance of around forty million minutes, even if most of us waste half of them sleeping, picking our noses or dozing off at work. The most important minute is your first. You have no choice about that one, but if it doesn't happen you can forget about the rest. There's not much you can do about your last minute either – it's going to tick by one of these days, whether you like it or not. What you do with the 39,999,998 in between is mostly up to you.

Monday 17 March 2003

How long can a normal human embryo be stored safely in cryopreservation? With its life on hold before it has even begun, at minus 196 degrees Celsius packed inside a carefully sealed "straw": (a) 10 minutes or so? (b) 24 hours maybe? Or (c) up to five years – if the conditions are right and the clinic staff know what they're doing?

Answer (c) is the one I have been led to believe, but even this is not strictly true. When the time comes, and if all parties agree (with the notable exception of the embryo itself, of course), it is quite acceptable to extend the storage period to 10 years, or even more in some countries.

With all the advances in reproductive medicine over the last two or three decades, many scientists now believe that frozen embryos can remain viable, potentially, for an indefinite period. In fact, the theoretical limit is thought to be around 10,000 years. By then the natural background radiation of the earth is likely to have damaged the embryo's DNA to such an extent that it would no longer be capable of growing and developing properly. Not to mention that the child would probably wake up to find the world inhabited by giant ants, killer robots and a whole load of dysfunctional people dressed in 1970s-style silver cloaks and jumpsuits, the likes of which are not normally seen outside of classic *Doctor Who* re-runs.

The UK's Human Fertilisation and Embryology Authority, snappily known as the HFEA among its friends, still caps the storage period at 10 years – I'm betting they have their reasons, and it isn't all to do with giant ants. The reality is, no one knows for certain how long frozen embryos can be stored safely and this limit is an attempt to protect children who might be born damaged in some unknown way after being cryopreserved as an embryo for longer than that.

We're not even two into our first five years just yet, so I shouldn't be worried. It's hardly the time to feel stressed about impending deadlines, but I can't shake the idea that the longer we leave all this, the riper those poor little fellas in the cooler will get. There can be a big difference between the "use by" and "best before" dates on pre-packaged food and it often depends on how good your fridge or freezer is.

I never thought to ask whether the embryology clinic's storage tank has a "three star" or a "five star" compartment. I'm certainly hoping for something a bit more top of the range than the tired old Electrolux we have in our kitchen. However good it is, though, I am still struggling to understand how an extended stay inside in a tub full of liquid nitrogen can be anything but a bad thing.

I am painfully aware that the whole field of fertility research, especially when it comes to embryo storage, is still very new in the scheme of all things scientific. Doctors in Australia claimed their place in history as recently as 1984 with the birth of a girl called Zoe Leyland – the world's first human to negotiate her way through a successful pregnancy after being frozen as an embryo. But little Zoe, aged minus nine months, was frozen for only eight weeks or so before they turned the sun lamps on her – I've had yoghurts longer than that – and I don't suppose she missed too much while she was hanging about waiting.

Still, frozen is frozen, and I accept that the freezing and unfreezing of embryos must surely carry the strongest health warnings, however long the period in the middle. I have read about other successful pregnancies that have followed the thawing and transfer of embryos stashed away for almost a decade, but the thought of leaving ours tucked in the freezer for anything like that long makes me decidedly uneasy.

Based on the relatively sparse research available to me, it is hard to be certain that there are no long-term side effects from putting your family plans on ice like this, especially where a prolonged stay at minus 196 degrees Celsius is involved. I can't help thinking about the future impact on our child...

Sorry little Johnny's not done very well in class this year – he's "best before 2006" and you have to make allowances.

It chills me every time I consider the fact that any one of our potential children could have been tucking into his or her first birthday cake last December. By now, he or she could be 15 months old and toddling around the living room. Instead they are all stuck at the size of a pinhead and none of them have even started on anything as fundamental as trying to grow legs yet, let alone tried to walk on them.

I know it isn't always helpful to think like this and I do have a habit of over-analysing things. It's one of the reasons I am very good at putting off decisions. I like to go through all the facts carefully, researching everything in infinite detail. I have to be really sure before I commit myself to anything. In fact, if procrastination ever becomes an Olympic sport I will be right there, ready to compete for a gold medal. Obviously, when I say "right there", I'm exaggerating. I would have to think about it for a while. Weigh up the pros and cons, and then maybe…well, we'd have to wait and see.

My wife, by contrast, is normally the queen of the snap decision. Impulsive, almost to a fault. We make a good team, Lesley and me, because if we both took our time like I usually do, we'd never get anything done.

Although, as it happens, *never getting anything done* is exactly where we have been for some while now. It is close to two years since Lesley's enforced stay at the hospital in Hammersmith. The physical scars are long gone, I am happy to say, but the emotional ones remain and it is still hard to talk about how either of us really feels and the choices we will have to make one of these days. We have had a few breakthroughs along the way of course – our heart-to-heart in Cyprus and two or three more in the last 12 months or so.

Our last real discussion on the subject was conducted via email back in January, for goodness sake – so it's still not easy!

While I fully respect Lesley's reluctance to pursue any further fertility treatment just yet and I understand her fears and concerns, I really want to do something with our embryos and put this thing to bed. The chances of success should we choose to continue are poor anyway. We both know that. But even if all we manage to do is draw a line under things, I am convinced that we will at last feel able to move on with our lives.

I think that means a life without children, but we have never really stopped to consider the alternatives in a serious and rational way. And the concept of adoption seems so alien to both of us right now that even talking about it would probably feel like a betrayal of our frozen embryos.

So, through a process of communication that has either been electronic or occasional, we have tentatively agreed to target July or August this year to contact Mr Margara's fertility unit at Hammersmith…after yet another international jaunt. Lesley wanted the Maldives this time, but we settled on Cuba, bearing in mind the cost of a spectacular new addition we have made at the back of our house. We call it a conservatory, but our friend Andy has already christened it the "Ballroom".

Not that we can actually afford our grand construction or the holiday, let alone both, but these minor details mean very little to us these days. Our perspective has changed. Which, on balance, is probably a good thing. Especially today.

Lesley and I are both home early from work as planned. All our conservatory furniture is due to be delivered later. We have been excited for a while about the completion and formal opening of our own little Crystal Palace and we had made special arrangements to work from home this afternoon, so that we could be here when everything arrived. As it turns out, we needn't have bothered.

Both of us work at the UK head office of a struggling electrical retail group. Home of the out-of-stock laptop and cut price toaster and kettle combos, among many other electrical items you can probably pick up cheaper and more conveniently at your local supermarket these days.

I've been there eight years, Lesley just over one. As of this morning, neither of us has a job any more, along with more than 400 of our now former colleagues. That's both our family incomes gone in one fell swoop – we should be devastated. At the very least we should be angry and bitter.

But our perspective has changed.

I'd be lying if I said that the thought of no job combined with the £26,000 we've just added to the mortgage to cover the cost of our beloved new conservatory didn't send the tiniest shiver down my spine when I got home today. But I can dismiss it. There are more important things in life than jobs, houses and even conservatories. All of them can be replaced or done without for a while. There are some things that can't. The events of 2001 proved that to both of us.

So what has happened to us this morning is not important at all – it's a minor setback in the scheme of things. We can handle trivial stuff like this, no sweat.

Wednesday 15 September 2004

I park up and run round the other side of the car to open the door for Lesley. She steps out, a blank expression on her face. It's not an unhappy expression, just devoid of all emotion. We link arms and walk slowly towards the entrance.

'Welcome to...' I read the sign silently, but I can hardly believe we are here.

We are back at our local private hospital after more than three years. Three long years of agonising, soul searching, confusion and pain. Three years of uncertainty and frustration. I am a jumble of conflicting emotions as we stand at the door, so I can only begin to imagine how my wife is feeling right now. Lesley's last memory of this place was leaving in the back of an ambulance. It's a tough image to shake, even after all this time. So I'm quite relieved as she strolls, reasonably casually, into the hospital's reception area.

'We have a specialist appointment on the Matthews Wing,' Lesley tells the woman on reception.

By which she means we have come to see our IVF consultant at the fertility unit. They are very discreet about the f-word around here.

'Have you been here before?' asks the receptionist.

Oh yes.

She waves us on with a bright smile, and we walk a familiar path down the modern corridors of the hospital towards the original part of the building at the back. The Matthews Wing is the oldest part of the hospital – it has low ceilings and super-thick walls, giving it an ambience all of its own. For Lesley and me today, though, there is a sense of unreality about the place. I feel an odd air of detachment as I help myself to a coffee from their machine and both of us sit down in the waiting area.

There is a warm welcome from everyone here, although I detect a little nervousness around us too. It is great to see Julia, the lead practice nurse, and Karen, the doctor in charge of the fertility unit. They are certainly delighted to see us after all this time, and that helps to put us at ease. The only one missing today is Wendy, who we learn is on maternity leave, which must feel a bit like taking her work home with her.

Julia and Karen soon return to their tasks at hand and we are left to review the room, silently reading the notices and leaflets pinned to the wall. Many of them are instantly recognisable and it's a bit like we have walked through a door to April 2001. Nothing much has changed here since our last visit, which is somehow reassuring and disturbing at the same time. The fact that we are here at all feels significant – like we have finally made a very important decision.

Except we haven't.

I suppose this should be one year ago, and we should be sitting in Mr Margara's waiting room down at

Hammersmith. We had a plan back then, something to aim for. We both had new jobs, we had enjoyed a great fortnight's holiday in Cuba and our brand new conservatory was proving to be just the fortress of solitude and peace that we needed from time to time. We were facing up to our situation, we had an understanding and everything was clicking into place. What happened to all that?

Where have the last 12 months gone?

We weren't ready back then – that's the long and the short of it. *Neither of us.* We're still not ready now, but we're working on it. That's why we're at the hospital today.

A number of things have become clear to us over the past few months. First and foremost, we know that when we do this thing, that will be it. All our remaining hopes and dreams of having children depend on this. There are six frozen embryos between us and the end of the fertility road. Six sides of the same dice, with no guarantee that any of them will land face up. If this next stage of treatment fails, whenever it happens, we are out of options and any chance of us starting our own family will be finished forever.

So what about surrogacy, egg donation, even adoption? All of these are the helpful suggestions of our well-meaning friends and family, and I'd be lying if I said that none of these hold any kind of interest for me. But it's *no, no and no.* That's where we are right now. We have been through enough with our couple of IVF attempts, the serious threat to Lesley's life, not to mention the slightly less complicated, but equally doomed, IUI attempts and the years of trying (and crying) that came before that. If it's not to be, we will just have to come to terms with it.

You hear of couples somehow surviving a dozen or more unsuccessful IVF cycles, with a few failed surrogacy attempts thrown in for good measure. It is hard to imagine all the heartache and how hard your life must become when you just don't know when to stop. We have done what we can, there can be no regrets from here on.

So when we do this thing we have to be ready and it has to be right for both of us. It also has to happen somewhere we are comfortable. Whatever emotions are stirred in us by our local private hospital and by the one down at Hammersmith, in a straight fight we know there can be only one winner.

Last year, we had gone as far as asking the team at the embryology clinic in London to prepare our little "popsicles" for a journey to Mr Margara's clinic. The jovial comedy embryologist was in fine form that day, reassuring us that our embryos had indeed been behaving themselves in their frozen playpen. We only had to say the word and they'd be on their way to Hammersmith in a "jiffy". By which I hoped that he meant they'd be there *quickly*, as I was expecting a rather sturdier container than a padded envelope to transport our precious cargo.

Not that it really mattered. Apart from reminding us that the embryos still existed, it was a pointless phone call. Mr Jolly's latest comedy turn was wasted on us and the transfer across London was never going to happen. We had already begun to realise that the Hammersmith solution was never going to work for us.

It's not that we had any hang-ups about the place, and we will be eternally grateful to Mr Margara and the team for getting us through the darkest weeks of our lives. But travelling to and from the hospital was just too much hassle. It was simply impractical for us to continue with our fertility treatment at Hammersmith, 30 or more miles from home.

This realisation left us with just two options: do nothing, or do what had seemed unthinkable only two years earlier...

So we did nothing. Except try to live our normal lives for a bit. I got used to my new job in the City, working for a high street bank, where I seem to spend nearly all of my time working out how to tell people they are being outsourced or made redundant. All wonderful experience, should I ever apply for a job as the Grim Reaper, or pretty much any kind of role in Human Resources. Meanwhile Lesley has become an indispensable member of the small team at a local Chartered Surveyor.

Our friend Ellen came to visit, under happier circumstances than last time, and we took her to see *The Phantom of the Opera* in the West End of London. It was all part of our efforts to make up for missing out on *The Witches of Eastwick* during her previous visit – although I came very close to undermining everything when I nodded off three times amid the screeching and the clattering. But Ellen enjoyed the show, and that's what mattered. We owe her so much.

And so it continued. Lesley and I did all the normal stuff people do and, on the whole, it felt good. The stresses and strains that had taken over so much of our lives slowly drifted into the background. Everything seemed like it was before.

Until now.

What had seemed unthinkable has not just been thought, but brought to life. Although we are not here today to conclude our treatment. Not yet, anyway. That might have been a step too far. Certainly too big a step for us to take in one go. Instead, we are here to ask our IVF consultant to treat Lesley for something called "cystic hyperplasia" – a condition that can affect the womb and is a typical symptom of polycystic ovarian syndrome (PCOS).

Between all these ovarian syndromes, hyper-this and hyper-that, cysts and polycysts, I am beginning to lose count here. What we know is that if the cystic hyperplasia is left untreated it represents a long-term cancer risk. And, coincidentally, it would definitely need to be sorted out well in advance of any embryo transfers, when or if the time is right.

The consultant is his usual calm and assured self when we get in to see him – he knows exactly what to do. The only difference I pick up on this afternoon is a sense of familiarity, a connection that didn't quite exist before. Back then we were couple number whatever, part of a long string of visitors to the fertility unit. Today we are Lesley and Mike, you know, *that* couple. The ones who…well, they've come back.

When we arrive home, we are more than a little emotionally drained, but well satisfied with the consultant's suggestions for treatment. He has put Lesley on a course of tablets and in a couple of months he will perform a routine "laparoscopy" to sort out the problem. This is our focus – this is what today has been all about and nothing else.

Who are we trying to kid?

Neither of us dares to say it, but the decision has been made. We *both* know it. The day is coming when we will be back at the same hospital and so will our embryos. Everything that happens after that will depend on the roll of the dice.

13

Harley Street

Patience is a virtue I have very little time for these days. If I want to delay something I am more than capable of doing it all by myself, without any outside intervention. But life, like many of Britain's railways, has a habit of dropping mostly unexplained obstacles on the tracks ahead of you. The wrong kind of snow, a puma on the line, or a good old-fashioned points failure – they're all likely to delay your journey, or if you're really unlucky, send you on an expected detour to the back of beyond. The trick is to never give up, ignore life's published timetables and, wherever you can, make up your own rules. You'll end up doing just as much waiting around as anyone else, but you'll feel better about it – I know I do.

Wednesday 2 March 2005

There are a few things we are used to coming round in cycles of four years. The football World Cup for instance, the Olympic Games, or the election of a new American President. Most of these events happen on a grand or even global scale and millions share the anticipation. What Lesley and I are about to do is a small thing, of little consequence to most of these people, but it has still taken us almost four years to get here.

After several visits to the Matthews Wing since September – including a day for Lesley in one of their smart private rooms in January, when she went in for her laparoscopy – we are feeling sufficiently re-acclimatised to the place and (just about) ready for our final roll (or two) of the dice. It's an odd feeling for both of us. I can feel any certainty I have about where we are heading draining away fast. Suddenly it is hard to imagine what life will be like in a few months' time, whether or not we succeed in what we are about to do.

Meanwhile, Lesley is coping remarkably well, but I feel extremely guilty for encouraging her to go ahead with all this. It is never going to be easy, even if all the doctors are right and the health risks at this end of the fertility machine are small to non-existent. We have to trust them, but even four-year-old memories can keep you awake at night.

As is so often the best strategy, we need to keep busy and there are plenty of things we have to do first if we want to get back into this particular game. There are travel plans to make for our precious "popsicles" down at the embryology clinic for one thing, and already that's not really going too well. We contacted the team down in Harley Street a few days ago to discuss transferring our embryos to our local hospital, but it seems that Mr Jolly the comedy embryologist is long gone. Instead, we were met with a considerably more frosty reception. They simply told us they would look into it and make the necessary arrangements.

'The courier will cost £90…'

Now wait a minute! We are not entrusting our embryos to some courier. Not after all we've been through.

We told them as much and explained that we would

come down to the clinic and pick up the embryos in person. That has always been the firm recommendation from Karen, the doctor in charge of the fertility unit on the Matthews Wing. This is a part of the process that is too important to be left to chance, or the whims of a man driving a white van. For all we know, he might specialise in anything from Amazon book deliveries to transporting spare hearts required for urgent surgery.

Who can say how a handful of embryos might fit into those kinds of priorities?

The embryologist we spoke to promised to inform us when we could make the collection, but we heard nothing and we finally received a call from Karen yesterday.

We were expecting her to call us, as she is waiting for an update on our embryos. What we weren't expecting was to hear that someone from the embryology clinic had been in touch with Karen directly. All they told her, however, is that we owe an outstanding balance of £600 for the embryo storage. Which was news to us, and I'm puzzled as to why they didn't mention this £600 when we spoke to them ourselves. It's not as if we are sitting on any unpaid invoices.

I remember rejecting a bill for more than that from our local hospital when Lesley was still seriously ill down at Hammersmith, but that has nothing to do with any of this. The only invoice we have ever had from the Harley Street clinic was for the freezing of our six embryos and their first year's storage. That bill was for £200 and we paid it in full at the time. It doesn't seem at all unreasonable that by now we might owe them some more cash, but they have never asked us for any.

What has me just a little peeved is the fact that they have: (a) disclosed our private financial information to a third party, (b) intimated to that third party that we have wilfully withheld payment for some reason, and (c) suggested that our embryos somehow belong to them until we pay up. And all this without even speaking to us.

This sudden shift in attitude seemed very strange, so we sent an email to the embryology clinic to clarify things.

When we received their reply this morning, they were very clear, instructing us in no uncertain terms that the £600 'must be paid prior to the release of your embryos'. And that was it – what amounted to a ransom note telling us our embryos will be held hostage in the freezers at their clinic until we hand over a sum of money they appear to have plucked out of the air.

Now, I'm no expert in embryo law, child abduction, or the finer points of kidnapping and ransom negotiation, but I have a gut feeling that the stance they have taken here might not be entirely legal. I really want to gather an armed response team and storm their building – let them know they are asking for trouble if they want to play this kind of game with us. Instead we drop them another email, express our dismay at their bullying tactics and *instruct them* to send us these missing invoices immediately. We have no issue with paying what's due, it's the heavy-handed and impersonal way we are being treated that plays havoc with the stress levels.

Do they *really* think we can't be trusted? That as soon as we have our embryos, we will simply run off to Brazil or somewhere and never be heard from again?

Sensitivity and discretion are important qualities in the medical profession, especially where money and fertility are involved. Right now, I don't know what to think about the embryology clinic. They've gone from comedians to extortionists in the space of a few days. Lesley and I just want to resolve this ridiculous situation and move on to the important matters ahead of us.

Monday 14 March 2005

Parking a car anywhere near Harley Street has never been the easiest task. There are lines of parking meters on either side of all the streets and side roads and just about all of them are occupied. All the time.

We have arrived just before 11 o'clock this morning to collect our precious "popsicles" in person from the embryology clinic. We paid their invoice the moment they sent it through to us – three years storage at £200 a year. Fair enough. As far as Lesley and I are concerned, that was £600 well spent for our last chance at parenthood. It's cost us far more than money to get to this point.

I am actually nervous just trying to park the car; who knows what I will feel like when we have the embryos tucked inside their special strongbox and are heading back to the fertility unit with the poor little fellas on board. I finally find a space to squeeze into, just around the corner from Harley Street, and we dash through the clinic's door in time for our 11am appointment with destiny.

If the receptionist recognises us as the "storage fee renegades" of a couple of weeks back, she doesn't let on and greets us warmly, then asks us to take a seat in the waiting room. Within a few minutes, one of the embryologists appears to retrieve our strongbox. So far so good, it won't be long now and we'll be on our way.

By 11.55 I am beginning to panic. Not because there is no sign of the embryologist with our precious cargo, but due to the fact that I have foolishly fed the meter with just enough money for an hour's parking. I had imagined we would be in and out of here pretty quickly. This whole digging embryo straws out of the freezer routine obviously takes a bit longer than I had anticipated.

Certain that the moment I rush out to the car, someone will turn up, strongbox in hand, I hang on as long as I can, but on the hour I give in. The last thing we need right now is for the car to get towed away or clamped. That really would take the difficulty factor attached to our day up a notch or two.

Of course, it's not as simple as pumping a few more

coins into the meter. Oh no. I have to move my car to an entirely different spot and start all over again. It can't even be in the same run of spaces, the local parking rules are clear, so I swing round the block a couple of times until I find another bay, this time on Harley Street itself. It's at times like this that I really miss that broken ticket machine outside Wormwood Scrubs. How come there's never a disgruntled ex-con around when you need one?

I feed the meter, but even as I walk back into the clinic, I am cursing my own stupidity. I have put another hour on the clock, which should be ample to conclude our affairs here. But this is so not the right time to tempt fate…

Sure enough, when I rejoin Lesley in the waiting room, nothing's changed. If I expected my absence to trigger some chain of events, like the way someone always scores a goal when you pop to the toilet during a football match, then I am sadly disappointed. Lesley has just checked with the girl on reception, but she is no wiser as to what is happening.

I give it 10 more minutes, then sneak downstairs to where I know the embryology team do all their work. There is little sign of life, so I skulk back up to see Lesley, bemused by the lack of apparent activity or information.

'Do you think they're still annoyed with us about the invoice thing?' offers Lesley.

I shrug. Maybe, but not as angry as I will be if they think making us hang around like this is some kind of payback for something that was entirely their fault in the first place. The minutes tick by and I am just about ready to go back into the reception and start causing a scene, when I realise it is very nearly one o'clock.

Damn it – I'm going to have to move the car again.

I dash outside and jump into the car, just strides ahead of an approaching traffic warden. There are loads of them round here, always on the prowl, so there's very little margin for error on the meter front. By now, though,

Harley Street is teeming with lunchtime traffic and it's an even bigger nightmare finding somewhere else to park. When I spot an empty bay, I'm more than a couple of streets away from the clinic, but it will have to do.

Back inside, I find Lesley talking to the receptionist and she has an update for us at last. It seems that the lead embryologist wasn't available when we arrived and they've had some kind of mix-up over times and over who had to do what. They are very sorry for keeping us waiting and someone will be with us in just a few minutes. Lesley and I let out a collective sigh. We should have known this was never going to be simple. At least they are making the right noises now, so we head back to the waiting room and drop into a couple of chairs.

I can still feel the tension growing, as we sit here quietly, staring at the clock. Fifteen minutes pass and I can't shake the idea that someone's going to appear in a minute and offer me and Lesley a couple of choc-ices they've turned up during the search for our embryos. Consolation prizes in exchange for our little "popsicles", who have obviously beaten the staff here in today's unscheduled game of hide and seek. My dreams of iced dairy products are suddenly broken when the lead embryologist finally walks into the waiting room, carrying the strongbox.

'Sorry about the wait,' she says and hands me the box.

The wait? Is that what you call it? Almost two-and-a-half miserable hours? And all that messing about with the car?

Of course, the only thing either of us manages to say is 'thank you' and the embryologist slips away quickly, clearly uncomfortable. It doesn't matter now anyway, we have what we came here for.

Driving back with the embryos on board, Lesley and I can't quite believe what a mentally tiring morning we have had. First getting our heads around what we were about to do, then having to wait so long to complete what we thought was sure to be the easiest bit. Who would have thought a courier's job would be this tricky? At least we didn't have to waste any more time proving who we were and signing any paperwork to confirm we had collected our embryos. Although, on reflection, you would think someone might have asked us about both these things.

Monday 21 March 2005
It took us about an hour to reach our local hospital and drop off the embryos with Karen last Monday. It was annoying that this supposedly simple task had turned into such a trial, but it felt really good to get it out of the way. We had an unexpected sense of achievement, especially after all that waiting around on Harley Street.

We had already set a date with our IVF consultant for the embryo transfer this week and the regulation of Lesley's hormonal cycle was all going to plan. So we knew we would be ready, and with the "straws" safely in the care of the team at the fertility unit, we were just about good to go.

Of course, life couldn't be that simple, or that kind. A couple of days of eager anticipation after dropping off the embryos, everything started unravelling again. Karen called us last Wednesday, late afternoon. We could tell there was something wrong. Normally, she has a voice that smiles at you through the telephone. Last Wednesday, Karen's hushed, serious tone betrayed her concerns when she explained that our embryos had not been accompanied by all the necessary paperwork, as required according to the HFEA guidelines. The fact that there were only three "straws" in the strongbox when it arrived troubled her too.

'I raised all this straight away with the embryology clinic,' Karen went on, choosing her words carefully. 'They haven't been able to resolve the issue.'

In the absence of this paperwork, there was no way for Karen to know whether each of our "straws" contained two embryos frozen together, or just one on its own. It is not uncommon for embryos to be frozen in pairs, so we reasoned that our problem was probably just one of inefficient bureaucracy and that someone had simply mislaid the necessary papers.

Assuming that these are actually our embryos at all...

Fortunately, Karen was able to quash any possible fears we had on that front, as all three "straws" were clearly marked with our name and the date of freezing. It's just that our friend Mr Jolly, the comedy embryologist, or one of his colleagues at the time, had either forgotten to write up all the appropriate notes, or had managed to lose them down the back of a filing cabinet somewhere in the bowels of the clinic.

The long wait in Harley Street was starting to make more sense to us, but we had to remain optimistic that everything would be fine, even if Karen's grave tone indicated otherwise. The whole idea that suddenly we might not have all of our embryos after all was too much for me to take in right away. Instead, I found myself making bizarre comparisons to the *Schrödinger's Cat Paradox*. You know the one – you put a cat in a box and expose it to a radioactive isotope with the potential to deliver a lethal dose of radiation. Until you open the box, the cat is both alive and dead, or neither one nor the other. *Theoretically.* No one's ever performed the experiment, of course, it is a paradox of Quantum Physics that has taxed the brains of (and I suspect mildly amused) scientists and philosophers for years.

Except now we have our very own version of the unfortunate cat. Until we start thawing out our "straws", ready for this week's embryo transfer, we have three or we have six. Or is it: we have three *and* we have six? I don't know. It has less to do with Quantum Physics than it does with some numpty failing to complete the paperwork correctly, but it feels like a big enough paradox to Lesley and me.

The difference between having six viable embryos and just three for our continuing IVF treatment is immense – at least for us and our hopes of ever starting a family. The guidelines fertility clinics work to are strict and this means that a specialist is restricted to using no more than two embryos during any single treatment cycle. Assuming they all survive the thawing process – not such a long shot, but hardly guaranteed – six embryos gives you a pretty good chance of three attempts at conception. You simply thaw out two at a time, probably over a period of months, and hope for the best. Having just three embryos changes everything. Once you've thawed out two, you might as well take a look at the other one, pick the best two out of three and launch them into the womb with your fingers crossed. That effectively cuts your chances down to just one decent shot.

Whatever the truth is, we'll know soon enough. They are thawing out the embryos at the fertility unit today.

To be honest, the content of Karen's call when it comes this afternoon is no surprise to us. The first "straw" contained a single embryo and so did the second. The third was the same and that was it. *Confirmed.* We are three embryos light. Our three possible chances have become one. Just like that. Any other time and I'd be making some tired old quip about this really being the "final straw". As it is, I'm speechless.

After letting us know, Karen has to follow all the standard protocols, as if this happens every day (though I'm absolutely sure it doesn't) – so she alerts the embryology clinic and contacts the HFEA. She also advises us to report the issue to the authorities ourselves and gives us a contact to write to.

However, we are under no illusions that the HFEA will have the power or even the inclination to intervene on our behalf, or to take any action over any dispute we might become involved in. That's not what they do – these guys are regulators, not patient advocates. What the HFEA will do, we are told, is 'investigate on its own behalf when there is evidence of a breach, or potential breach, of the Human Fertilisation and Embryology Act or Code of Practice.' In other words, they're about upholding the rules, not fighting for justice.

By the time I have finished drafting my letter to the HFEA, I'm past caring what their remit might be. I have run through all of today's events and the couple of weeks leading up to them. My initial shock of earlier has developed steadily into a quiet and remarkably restrained form of rage. I tell them in the letter how very upsetting this has all been for Lesley and me. How our stress levels were already high enough before this latest revelation. And how we want them to investigate this "breach", or whatever they want to call it, as a matter of urgency.

Oh, and if it wouldn't be too much trouble, perhaps they could try and help us find our missing embryos...

As I read back the letter, the calm words belie my growing anger and I can feel myself shaking. We have pinned our hopes on this day for so long. Our embryos had been stashed away safely for all that time. Or so we thought. After everything. After four long years of waiting and mustering up the courage to press on.

After every-damn-thing that happened to Lesley.

Now this? Some careless refrigerator attendant has managed to lose three of our embryos and, conveniently, all the related paperwork. Comedy embryologists there may be, but I didn't see this punchline coming.

14

Lost

After years in a cold, dark place, all you really want to hear is another human voice. You long to see a friendly face, as you hug yourself for warmth and prepare for the sunlight. It's not as if your rescuer even has to smile. Just to have someone acknowledge your existence would be something. One or two steps further and you will be free...you know that, but the exit still seems so far away. Then you're out, and it's only now that you truly understand how desperate things have become. That cold prison suddenly seems quite cosy when you survey the frozen wasteland, stretching out for miles around you. Your mind can barely register just how lost you are...and the fact that no one's going to find you here. Ever.

Wednesday 23 March 2005
Today's the day. Everything depends on a couple of carefully defrosted clumps of human cells, packed with all the "peopley" goodness it takes to grow a baby. We know our chances are probably languishing somewhere on the

wrong side of 15 per cent. At least we haven't hit the big fat zero. Not yet, anyway.

Two of our three embryos survived the thaw on Monday and have prospered sufficiently under the tender care of Dr Karen Goode on the Matthews Wing. The third fared slightly less well, so in line with HFEA rules the unfortunate little tyke has missed the cut and it's all over for him now.

We check into the fertility unit at the hospital just before 11am with a degree of hope. We have to. Nothing about the day's events will be dignified for Lesley, but the embryo transfer is quite routine. As routine as anything can be anyway, when you are lying on the doctor's treatment table with your feet up in the air in stirrups. We keep telling ourselves that the procedure *can* be successful. And as no one knows where our other three embryos are right now, it had better be.

When we wrote our letter to the HFEA a couple of days ago, we sent a copy to the embryology clinic too. One of the embryologists there called us right away to express their concern and to reassure us that they are taking the matter very seriously. They will be meeting with the HFEA towards the end of the month to discuss the situation. That will give the staff at the clinic time to review their procedures and try to work out what went wrong. To be honest though, all we want them to do is locate our missing embryos, even if that already looks to be the unlikeliest outcome of all.

By the time they have their meeting, one thing is for certain – we will know whether today's attempt has worked. Lesley might be pregnant by then and the lost embryos will seem an irrelevance, albeit one that will pop into our heads from time to time and make us wonder what might have been…and prompt us to keep on asking where on earth they could have disappeared to anyway?

On the other hand, if the embryo transfer doesn't take,

I'm not sure where we'll be. Or exactly what will be popping into our heads over the next few days, weeks, months or years. I had expected this to be the end. Time to move on to whatever life has in store for us next. Thanks to a bureaucratic mix-up of inexcusable proportions, we are now in danger of stalling again – unsure whether we might still have a shot at parenthood, even if this latest treatment fails.

Right now, there's not much more Lesley and I can do apart from lie back, think of England and hope for the best of British luck. At this precise moment, Lesley is doing most of the lying back and I'm trying to focus on hoping for the best. Despite the undoubted pressure that places on me in the areas of crossing fingers, purchasing lucky heather or chopping off rabbit's feet and mounting them on a handy key chain, I am under no illusions that I have the cushy end of the deal.

What we can share, very shortly, is the agonising wait to see whether all of this effort has been worth it.

Thursday 14 July 2005

A licensee is someone I would expect to find running a public house, where they are licensed to sell real ales and other intoxicating liquors. Embryology clinics have licensees too, minus all that stuff about the alcoholic beverages presumably, although I'm beginning to wonder.

Just like at your local pub, the "Nominal Licensee" at an embryology clinic is the one with his name above the door. You may never meet him, but he's the formal holder of the clinic's licence to operate and, in effect, all the fertility treatment carried out there is done on his behalf. It's quite a responsibility at the best of times. But when things go wrong, the Nominal Licensee is the one who has to defend the clinic's honour, deal with the HFEA inspectors and, if possible, put things right. Lesley and I are off to Harley Street again today, to meet the Nominal Licensee of the embryology clinic we have been dealing with there – and the man we hope can put things right for us.

It is now more than three months since Lesley took the pregnancy test, following the embryo transfer in March. Our hopes were never that high, but surely we'd earned a happy ending somewhere along the line? We only had to get lucky this one time and it would have been "job done" at last. We deserved that much, didn't we?

The test was negative.

So here we are, back at the clinic trying to track down our three missing embryos – in a last desperate effort to draw a line under everything. There is no way we can move on without doing this, although the whole attempt has an air of failure about it, even before it has properly begun.

The Head of Clinical Governance at the HFEA has already prepared us for the worst in one of her first letters in response to our complaint:

'I note you are expecting the centre to provide you with a report on the progress they are making in recovering your lost embryos.'

'I'm not sure we're really expecting anything of the sort, but what else do you expect us to ask for?'

'While I do not want to be unduly pessimistic or cause you unnecessary worry, I feel I should raise your awareness of the possibility that the centre may not be able to find your embryos.'

'No kidding, huh, but we have to try.'

The last time we were at Harley Street, they had us waiting around for hours. Today we are whisked off to the Licensee's office within minutes of our arrival. Our path to this meeting has been considerably more torturous, however, as whatever's been going on between the HFEA and the clinic has been pretty much invisible to us. And it has taken an unbearably long time. When we chased them both up for a response in May and June, there was very little news from either party. One of the inspectors at the

HFEA called with a few more questions though, and explained that they would be carrying out an audit of the embryology clinic shortly.

So at least we had something to cling onto. If we had any chance of success in all this, or even of getting some answers that might help us deal with whatever's happened, then a full audit of the clinic's embryo storage tanks had to be the place to start.

When we finally heard from someone at the clinic itself, it was our first contact with their Nominal Licensee. He introduced himself as such on the telephone and, while I did catch his name, I was so intrigued by the job title that I really wanted to call him NL, in deference to the medical world's fondness for abbreviation. He had a soft but reassuring voice and I noticed that he spoke with a carefully measured tone. The first thing he stressed was how sorry he was to hear that our recent procedure hadn't worked.

He would say that, wouldn't he?

Well, of course – had the embryo transfer been successful it would have probably got him off the hook. But for all our natural scepticism, we could tell NL was sincere. He struck us as a thoughtful man, a man of considerable experience, and he was definitely keen to meet up with us once the HFEA investigation of the clinic was complete. Even so, as we walk into the small office the Nominal Licensee is using today, I am ready to give him a pretty stern talking to.

Our constant badgering of the HFEA has given us the impression that the investigation turned up nothing significant, although we are still awaiting their official feedback. They must have turned this place upside down, so if there really was no sign of our embryos or the paperwork that should have been filed on their behalf, we need to find out why.

Usually, when you are in situations like this, all the

power sits with the doctor or consultant. You are subject to their every whim – dependent on their knowledge and experience, their patience and usually the time available. Today, we are the ones with the power. NL is the one with some explaining to do, and I am determined that this time things will be different…

Except they're not.

There's a lump in my throat and my confidence fades with every footstep. I can feel the air being sucked out of my lungs and my throat is so dry that when we shake hands, my response to the doctor's friendly greeting is cracked and barely audible. NL is not an intimidating man, but the position we are in *is*. We have no idea what he is going to say to us – we have no idea what he can *possibly* say – but we're here now and ready to listen.

NL introduces himself properly and goes through all the social niceties. He starts by telling us a bit about his background and his role at the clinic. He is one of the most experienced infertility specialists in the UK. He worked at the University of Cambridge when the first IVF baby was born in 1978 and he has been a senior director of a large IVF & Fertility Trust in the UK since 1986. When the embryology clinic we are familiar with became one of his Trust's centres just a couple of years ago, he also took on the role of Nominal Licensee here.

The doctor is compelling, full of sympathy for us and well spoken. To my surprise, I find myself warming to him. But I still want to burn his clinic to the ground. He is quick to point out that the relatively recent involvement of the Trust means that the clinic has come under new management. In fact, all of the key people who ran the place when we were here four years ago have now moved on.

I am starting to get a feel for where this is heading.

'We had the auditors in from the HFEA and they didn't find anything amiss,' he shrugs.

'*Tell me something I don't know…*'

'The only conclusion I can draw from our investigation is that only three of your embryos were cryopreserved in the first place. It seems likeliest that the other three didn't survive the freezing process.'

'... *but not that.*'

This is another of those hold-it-right-there moments I am becoming all too familiar with in relation to our fertility treatment.

Only three of our embryos were cryopreserved in the first place? The other three didn't survive the freezing process? What kind of nonsense is this?

I look him up and down, almost nodding as this statement sinks in and the doctor continues by telling us about the problems that can arise during the cryopreservation process. He thinks this could explain why all six embryos identified for freezing were not preserved successfully.

Nobody says anything for almost a minute. Slowly, I realise he's *not* kidding. *This is it.* This is what we came here for today. This is his explanation. Our embryos have not been lost at all... *they never even existed.* And there's no one still here at the clinic who can confirm the facts either way.

I'm not buying it, but it's hard to take on NL's logic in the stuffy confines of this meeting room. Finally, he breaks the silence, once again expressing his sympathy for what we are going through. He reminds us that the clinic has changed hands since the almighty goof that landed us all in this position, but insists that he would like to put things right. And he has a proposal for us.

'Given what has happened, our trustees have authorised me to offer you an IVF treatment cycle at any one of our centres, free of charge, under one of our top specialists...'

I am open mouthed as I listen to what the doctor is suggesting and, glancing sideways, I can see the blood draining from Lesley's face.

So before he can continue, I try to explain why we can't

consider further treatment – under *any* circumstances. I tell him about the OHSS, about Lesley's enforced stay down at Hammersmith, and I tell him how hard a decision it was for us even to proceed with the embryo transfer back in May.

NL is unfazed. He has a cool and understated air about him and he is obviously used to dealing with difficult situations and, when necessary, difficult people like us. He is a fiercely intelligent man who knows his stuff, but I have the distinct feeling that he doesn't quite get where we are on this.

He is certainly sympathetic to Lesley's plight and can recall a patient of his who suffered from one of the first recorded cases of severe OHSS. This poor woman had spent a couple of nights in hospital at the time, and it had been very distressing. I try to interject and point out that Lesley's experiences have been in an entirely different ballpark to this woman's, but the doctor is keen to continue his pitch.

'Techniques in treating infertility have moved on a long way, even in the last four years,' he explains, and I am acutely aware that he is now just talking to me – it's as if Lesley has left the room. 'I can arrange a meeting for you with our most senior consultant. He can talk you through the new treatment protocols that significantly reduce the need for drugs and the risks of OHSS...'

Without even looking in Lesley's direction this time, I can tell her whole body is beginning to shake. I turn to her and my wife's face is a pale mask of horror. Then there are tears. Floods of tears. Tears born of anger, frustration, but most of all fear. She is a powder keg ready to blow, but is just about holding it together. Somehow.

The doctor stops talking mid-sentence and I see a flicker of alarm in his eyes. He is not quite sure what has just happened and looks to me for some help. I have none to give him. Lesley and I are together on this one. I put my arm around my wife's shoulders and comfort her the best I can. It takes Lesley a few minutes to regain her composure and NL just sits there, patiently waiting. His initial alarm has been replaced by practised concern. He has obviously seen all this before and knows only too well how emotional the fertility business can get at times.

'If I feel…like this…when you are just talking about it,' Lesley manages, having barely recovered her powers of speech, 'then imagine how I would feel…if we went ahead with any more…fertility treatment.'

The words almost stick in her throat.

NL nods sagely and I believe he has finally got the message. Further treatment is not an option. *Not under any circumstances.* With this avenue closed, there is not much more he can say to us, so we agree to end the meeting. We need to go away and think through what has been said today. If we would like to come back and talk further, the doctor kindly makes it clear that we will be made welcome. And, as he ushers us to the door, he reminds us that if we were to change our minds about further treatment here or at one of their other fertility centres, his offer would stand. Lesley shakes her head and gives me one of her looks on the way out. All I want to hear right now is what the team at the HFEA have to say about this.

We came into London on the train today to minimise the stress of the visit, so I call them on my mobile as we walk back to Marylebone station. I don't feel particularly talkative after the meeting we've just had, and the Inspector at the HFEA has very little to say for herself either. It boils down to this: while the missing paperwork is a technical breach of their guidelines, they have found nothing else during their investigation. No indication of wrongdoing, no sign of our missing embryos and, crucially, no hard evidence that they ever actually existed at all.

In effect, they are agreeing with the explanation offered to us this morning by NL. It's not a "known known", as the saying goes, but the likeliest "unknown known" in a pretty sparse field of reasonable or unreasonable speculations.

As we walk past Madame Tussaud's, Lesley points out one of those horribly over-priced cafes near to Baker Street underground station and suggests we stop for a coffee. Even from the outside, the quaint façade of a good, old fashioned, independently run vendor of hot and cold beverages and snacks is screaming "dodgy tourist trap" to me. This is the kind of place that has you applauding the fact that it is only a matter of time before it becomes another Starbucks. At least then, when you pay the big bucks for your skinny latte, you'll know exactly what you'll be getting for your money.

When I'm finished with the HFEA, I hang up the phone and we head inside. The Inspector has promised to put their detailed findings in writing to us shortly, but right now we need a drink and something to eat. I could do with something stronger than a coffee, but it's the best thing on offer and, having made our selections at the self-service counter, I hand over a twenty-pound note to the miserable man at the till.

You want to have a day like we're having, mate. Then you might have a reason for being so miserable.

We sit down and it's hard to find the right words. The only answers we are getting from anyone today raise fundamental questions about what we have believed to be true for the last four-and-a-bit years.

There were only ever three embryos.

Can we possibly believe that?

As we struggle with our late breakfast, one thing Lesley and I definitely agree on is that all this cannot be allowed to end here. Not over almost 14 quid's worth of ropey coffee and a couple of partially stale Danish pastries.

15

Questions

Are we there yet? What's up, doc? Who do you think you are? Some of my oldest and most reliable friends are questions. Why is the sky blue? Where did you get that hat? How much is that doggie in the window? The questions stick around long after the answers have waltzed in, shown off how very clever they are, taken a couple of bows and waltzed out again. When you think about it, life is not really about finding the "right" answers – that just leads to arguments and a world of unpleasantness. It's about asking the right questions. That's what drives us on, and sometimes questions are all we have.

Wednesday 10 August 2005

Thank goodness for Dr Karen Goode, that's all I can say. We waited for more than a fortnight for the HFEA to confirm their findings in a letter after our meeting down at Harley Street. Lesley called Karen at our local fertility unit right away to update her on what we had been told by NL, and now in writing by our contact at the HFEA:

'An examination of the laboratory records on the day

does suggest that six embryos were identified initially. However, it is probable that in fact a different number of embryos were frozen. Unfortunately the paperwork was not completed in full at the time, i.e. one box on the paperwork had not been completed, therefore the exact number remains unclear.'

Roll up, roll up, for the amazing missing embryos trick. Which cup are they under? Go on, take a guess. You're wrong! They were never there in the first place...

'Since that time, there have been a number of staff changes at the centre. It is the opinion of the current members of staff that failure to complete the box in the paperwork suggests to them that only three embryos were frozen at the time.'

In short, the HFEA's and the clinic's own investigations turned up nothing, all the key people involved have moved on, and there is no hard evidence that all six of our embryos were actually frozen at all. In other words – *go to jail, move directly to jail, do not pass "Go" and do not collect your three missing embryos.*

Karen listened quietly to what my wife was telling her. Something was clearly bothering her about all this – apart from all the obvious stuff that was definitely bothering us. She told Lesley that she needed to check a few things out and would call us back as soon as possible.

For our part, we didn't know what to think. Whether we were prepared to admit it or not, a genuine doubt had been raised in our minds about what can go wrong during the cryopreservation process. The difference between identifying six viable embryos for freezing and actually preserving them successfully might be a big deal for all we know. I mean, there have to be risks when you carry out a delicate procedure like that.

In a way, the HFEA's findings, or lack of them, have simply confirmed my deepest, darkest fears – the ones that have been bothering me since way before I ever heard the ominous phrase, "freeze all".

But Dr Goode is aptly named and, while we were fretting, she did some digging on our behalf. True to her word, she called us back to discuss things further and, just over a week later, we are meeting with her today.

It soon becomes clear that Karen is puzzled by the embryology clinic's and the HFEA's explanation – it just doesn't stack up with the science.

First off, she tells us a bit about "pronuclei" embryos. These little chaps are still fresh from the test tube or Petri dish – they're the ones with the little signs hanging off their back saying: "just fertilised". They get their name from the two pronuclei that (if you look very closely) can be seen in the cell, representing chromosomes from the mother and the father. If you really want to pinpoint where we all start out, then pronuclei is where it's at, man.

Pronuclei embryos are uncomplicated and robust fellows that can take almost anything you decide to throw at them. However, when you nurture them for two or three days, just as you would when preparing for an embryo transfer, they reach what is known as the "cleavage" stage. That's when they divide into a collection of several cells, becoming a whole lot more wobbly and vulnerable in the process – emphasising the precarious and often contradictory progression of new life at this microbiological level.

Freezing an embryo at the cleavage stage has its advantages. Crucially, you have a far better idea whether it is likely to develop into a viable embryo for transfer back to the patient. Obvious really, because it has already negotiated its first spurt of growth before you lock it away in the freezer.

Unfortunately, the freezing process is a tad riskier business at this stage, with all these cells around. There is a significant chance that an individual cell or two in the group might not survive. If this happens they'll take the rest down with them without a second thought – and the embryo's not going to make it.

That's why freezing so often takes place when the embryo is still pronuclei – especially, we are told, in cases where a risk of OHSS is indicated in the patient. Embryos are simple beasts at this point, living a frugal "pre-life" with little or nothing going on, but confident in the knowledge that they can survive almost any kind of mucking about. They are tightly packed bundles of "potential human" at their toughest. There is very little delicate matter of any kind involved and they are neatly enclosed inside what is known as a *nuclear membrane*. I'm not so sure about the "nuclear" bit, but it's actually quite a cosy and safe place to be. I'd hate to be the one to tell the little pre-humans that it's all downhill from here...

At the cleavage stage it is quite possible to identify half a dozen likely embryos and mess up the freezing of any number of them. These things happen. But, following an instruction to "freeze all", as in our case, things would never have got that far. Karen is in no doubt that our embryos were frozen at the pronuclei stage, when there is little or no chance of the cryopreservation failing.

We sit in silence for a few moments, trying to grasp the science and significance of what Karen has just run by us. But she isn't finished. There's the small matter of standard HFEA auditing procedures that doesn't quite add up either. The fact that the paperwork relating to our embryos is incomplete makes it very hard for us, the HFEA or the staff at the clinic to track them down – or even to prove that they ever existed. But it seems there may be another way.

New HFEA regulations came into force in 2001, requiring all registered clinics to carry out annual audits of the embryos they are holding in storage. This means that the embryology clinic is supposed to have a robust audit trail, telling them exactly how many of *our* embryos they were storing from the time they checked into their freezer tank back in 2001, and at an agreed point each year since.

As no one was even sure how many embryos were held in the three straws we collected from Harley Street, just a few months ago, it would be interesting to find out how they recorded this in the clinic's annual audits. Especially during that first couple of years when our old mate Mr Jolly kept telling us he was keeping an eye on the embryos and making sure they were behaving themselves.

All this has us thinking that our contacts at the HFEA and the embryology clinic have a few more questions to answer. More than that, this is surely enough to place a very large cloud of doubt over their most "probable explanation" that the embryos never existed. Then Karen produces her *coup de grace*.

She was checking through all of the files she holds on our case when she came across a letter and some documents, sent to her back in 2001. The letter was written on 8 June 2001 by the Deputy Medical Director of the embryology clinic and was accompanied by a "summary of treatment" form. On the form one of the embryologists had scribbled down the details of the "freeze all" carried out for us several days earlier. The scribbles confirmed Karen's earlier pronuclei assertion, while in the letter, the Deputy Medical Director's message was to the point:

'Mrs Butcher has recently undergone a transport ICSI treatment cycle at this clinic. 20 oocytes were received in the clinic on 21.5.01. 18 oocytes were suitable for ICSI and were injected using the ICSI technique.'

I remember it well...

'6 achieved fertilisation. All embryos were cryopreserved from this treatment cycle due to the risk of OHSS.'

Whatwasthat?

'6 achieved fertilisation. All embryos were cryopreserved from this treatment cycle due to the risk of OHSS.'

Lesley and I have to read these couple of sentences a

few more times before we can allow ourselves to believe our eyes. For a moment, it's as if we are looking at a top-secret memo explaining how the CIA trained a martian to assassinate JFK – it's that mind-blowing. This is *exactly* what we have been hoping to find. The letter is what everyone has been looking for. '*6 achieved fertilisation and all embryos were cryopreserved*' – that's what it says. In black and white.

It's a clear declaration from the then Deputy Medical Director at the embryology clinic, making a nonsense of the only explanation offered up to us so far. And this follows an investigation spearheaded by the experts who police the fertility business. Top professionals in their field who have taken almost three months to conclude that there is no evidence to support our wild and crazy idea that the three missing embryos had ever actually existed. Evidence that we now hold in our hands.

We have blown to bits their conclusion after some pretty minimal investigation of our own. And it didn't require Sherlock Holmes, Miss Marple or Inspector Morse to crack the case – just a call to Karen on the Matthews Wing and a relatively quick look through our own correspondence file there.

If the words "useless…" something-or-other passed my lips when I realised that no one had thought to look for this vital clue, then I apologise. We need those experts at the HFEA – now, more than ever. People who can investigate this incident properly and leave no icy nooks or crannies unexplored. We need some kind of resolution after more than four years of turmoil, because I know we can't fix this thing on our own.

And, yes, I am fully aware they are powerless to act *directly* on our behalf – but if not them, who else is there?

Saturday 20 August 2005
I've calmed down a bit since our meeting with Karen. I

came away ready to storm the HFEA's office in London and demand some action. I was even considering mounting a picket line outside the embryology clinic until they jolly well came up with some answers. But Lesley and I have talked things through several times since then. Various online fertility resources have proved useful too, confirming what we have been told about pronuclei embryos and filling in the gaps where the detail was obviously too much for us to take in on the day.

So we have taken our time to review the facts, carefully going over what we know and what we don't, doing our best to maintain a reasonable level of perspective. We have drafted letters to our contact at the HFEA and to the Nominal Licensee at the clinic. We want them to reopen their investigation and take another look through *all* the available evidence. One more time.

It's not as if we are fooling ourselves here. The chances of us following some intricately laid set of clues to all the answers and the hidden location of our last three embryos are slim to non-existent. But we have to try. If nothing else, we just want them to take us seriously.

I honestly believe that the other players in this little game share some if not all of the confusion and frustration we are feeling. If they had the answers, they would surely be only too keen to share them with us. And in truth, we're not looking for anyone to blame. We're way past that now. The situation we are facing has to be just as difficult and bewildering for NL, the rest of the staff at the embryology clinic and even the team of inspectors at the HFEA. Well, almost.

It is possible – or probable, or even overwhelmingly likely – that we will never uncover the truth about what has happened to our embryos. Neither Lesley nor I need anyone at the HFEA or the clinic to tell us that. We are that close to accepting the fact and drawing a big line under this part of our lives. But we can't – not just yet. Not until we are convinced that the HFEA and the embryologists have done absolutely everything they can to solve the mystery. And they certainly haven't done that yet.

16

The most toys

Some people say that material goods and wealth can't make you happy. That there is more to life and you should focus on the spiritual aspects. Well, Karma's great in principle, but don't rely on it when you're stuck in a traffic jam. Whatever they try to tell you, life's quite capable of kicking you in the teeth and bad things really do happen to good people. If the cards are stacked against you, all you can really do is bluff your way through, or fold at the appropriate moment. The trick is to stay in the game as long as you can, but there comes a time when you have to give in and move onto the next one. That's when you get to play by an entirely new set of rules.

Monday 24 October 2005

In the end, we wrote to just about everybody we could think of. Our letter to NL was copied to the HFEA, the clinic's senior embryologist and their current medical director. If I had any way of tracking them down, their former deputy medical director and even Mr Jolly, the comedy embryologist, would have been on my list as well, but who knows what has happened to those two? Perhaps they've gone missing too.

To their credit, the HFEA sat up and noticed right away. Almost immediately their lead inspector was in touch to say:

'The centre is due for a routine inspection on Thursday 6 October 2005. This gives the HFEA an opportunity to send a multi-disciplinary team to inspect the clinic, and to examine the records and circumstances around your complaint.'

'I was hoping you had done all this last time…'

'The team will also be able to interview a key member of staff who was absent during the recent incident inspection.'

'Now you're talking, chief inspector!'

'I will let you know the outcome in due course. Thank you for your patience.'

And as non-committal as all that was, it made us feel better. The key people at the HFEA had clearly read our letter. They had given it some thought and this was their response. They were not patronising us. Nor feeling sorry for us. No, their attitude was business-like, straightforward and their messages right on the button:

We're going back to have another look and, as it happens, yes – there is someone else we can talk to at the clinic. Of course, there's every chance we won't find anything, but it won't be for the lack of trying.

We could ask no more of them than that.

So when another letter from the HFEA drops on our doormat this morning, neither Lesley nor I are quite sure what to expect. Could fate possibly have one last twist in store for us, now that the investigation is finally over and the inspection team has had time to review its findings? Could this little envelope be the miracle we have not even dared hope for these past few weeks?

Well, of course not, but this is not the whitewash of three months ago, either. We read what they have to say:

'I can advise you that another inspection has taken place.'

'*Great – so what did you find out?*'

'The HFEA investigations have not provided sufficient evidence to say exactly what happened in your case.'

'*Not much then.*'

'There remains a degree of uncertainty around events on the day the embryos were frozen, as well as some uncertainty regarding the number of straws stored, and the preparation of the paperwork for the transfer of the embryos.'

And that's it – they haven't really turned up anything different from last time. We should be disappointed, but we're not. We don't want the most convenient answer anyone can give us. *We want the truth.* And we don't need anyone to tell us that we can't handle it. If the truth is that no one knows the answer, then we want someone to say that.

This latest letter has explained the HFEA's findings in a matter of fact way. This time there is no attempt to jump to the nearest and simplest conclusion. We are grateful for that and at the very least it makes us feel as if our complaint has been treated seriously this time.

While it is likely to be a formality, I am pleased to read on and learn that the inspection team is due to present its findings to the HFEA's Licence Committee when it meets early in 2006. This Committee has the power to revoke a centre's licence to operate, or to place certain conditions or restrictions on what they do or the way that they work. None of this will happen, of course, and I don't really want it to.

No one currently at the embryology clinic has done anything wrong, and there's nothing solid to pin on anyone four years ago either. I really don't care about any of that.

It's just reassuring to hear that this kind of sanction is actually a possibility.

The HFEA inspector's final message is the most important to us.

'I apologise that our multi-disciplinary team has nothing specific to report,' her letter concludes. 'However, the monitoring of the centre continues and we will let you know if more details come to light.'

The team at the HFEA are sorry. They don't feel sorry for us. They are just sorry they couldn't do more to help. Which is all we wanted to hear.

If we could hear the same thing from Nominal Licensee at the embryology clinic, then we might even be able to get past all this and crack on with the rest of our lives. Not for the first time on our frustrating and luckless IVF journey, all roads lead to Harley Street...

Wednesday 30 November 2005
We are due to have what is likely to be our last meeting with the Nominal Licensee at noon. High Noon. Our final showdown.

For some reason, I want it to be like the opening scene of *Once Upon a Time in the West*. Lurking in the background, NL is the brooding dark figure of Henry Fonda while, rather worryingly, Lesley and I both play the part of Claudia Cardinale – here to honour a promise to ourselves and put to rest a lost loved one. Our train arrives at Marylebone station and the hanging sign on platform 2 is swinging back and forth, metal screeching on metal as it does so. Nobody says a word.

Oddly reassured by my uncanny ability to conjure up a world of my own to live in, even in the most inappropriate of circumstances, I hail a taxi. We have waited a few weeks for this meeting, so today has a surreal aura around it that has fuelled my sense of melodrama. The delay was reasonable enough – they needed a bit of time at the clinic to tie up their end of the investigation once the HFEA report was in, and it has not been in our interest to rush anyone.

The "spaghetti western" landscape recedes as we make the short journey to the embryology clinic and by the time we push open the heavy door that leads to their reception desk I am psyched up and ready to go. There will be no surprises today. No one is kidding anyone about the possible outcomes. It's not about sympathetic smiles, or last minute reprieves. It definitely has nothing to do with retribution – and there's no place here for bitterness. Lesley and I have talked a lot about what we want from this meeting. Above all, we just want them to say they're sorry.

And we know what's already on the table. After our first meeting with NL, he confirmed his offer of further IVF treatment in writing. Given the circumstances, there is also no question of the clinic hanging on to the storage fees they so forcibly extracted from us recently. These will obviously be refunded to us. That much is written up in black and white too.

Our views haven't changed on the free treatment. The Trust's offer is a generous one – a full IVF cycle at one of their centres could set you back £10,000 easy – but it is of no use to us now. That door is firmly closed. So what do we really want from today?

Our embryos, but that's not going to happen.

An apology and all of our money back would be nice, then. Not just the storage fees, but also whatever we have effectively paid them for all the embryology and any expenses arising from the messing about that has come since. None of this will make us feel any better about what we have lost. Or what we have *potentially* lost. Or whatever it is we might possibly have potentially lost, had we had a bit more luck and things had worked out a whole lot differently. But it will help us to draw that big fat line under everything. We will be able to mourn our "loss" – however you want to categorise it – and move on.

Today's meeting is in a larger, much airier and lighter room. It feels as though we have gone up in the world, and that our persistence has earned us a place in the fertility world's Club Lounge, minus the peanuts, light snacks and complementary newspaper.

There is tension in the room, but it's not like before. The doctor is viewing us through different eyes. Once again, he is quite charming and invites us to sit down, but he knows us now and I can see we have his respect. Not just for what we've been through, but for how we have handled the situation. He would probably be a lot happier if he could have swept this whole mess under the carpet months ago, but if it bothers him, he doesn't show it.

And it seems that, at last, he is on the same page as we are. He presumes we don't wish to pursue any further IVF treatment and our nods tell him that he presumes right. With that out of the way, he tells us that he can't say exactly what happened. He goes over what the HFEA have already told us and we're all right with that.

We came here looking for answers, but he and we know he has none to give us. It's a tough thing for a doctor to admit. They have to maintain an air of authority and infallibility, it comes with the territory. But there are many possible explanations for what has happened to our embryos. Clinging to any single one of them would be an effort to fob us off and he knows it.

NL doesn't even try. He is straight with us and we know he has done everything he can to get to the bottom of this for us. Now, all he can do is try to square things. He can't give us answers and he can't give us free treatment, but he can give us our money (and maybe our lives) back. He tells us he will have his administrators go through our records and come up with the appropriate figure.

It's a bit like holding out for the jackpot and finding out all you've won is your bus fare home. We never wanted this outcome, but right now we'll take it. After everything we've been through – the IVF, the OHSS, the critical care at Hammersmith, the years of anguish and our recent disappointments – this is our consolation goal in a 5-1 thrashing. But we're still standing at the final whistle.

The meeting ends in something of a whirl and when we get up to leave, somewhat surprisingly, we get *exactly* what we came for. NL shakes my hand, then he turns to Lesley and grips her hand tightly.

'I really am so very sorry for what has happened,' he tells her with genuine feeling.

We have come to an understanding and it will be up to NL to handle things from here. We are both content that, barring the insignificant details around what we have agreed today, our business with his clinic is done.

As Lesley and I walk back to Marylebone, we chat quietly about what has been said and how it's all for the best. We notice the cafe near Madame Tussauds we stopped at the last time we came this way – and give it a wide berth. Just around the corner, on Baker Street itself, is a Costa Coffee franchise (Starbucks haven't taken over the whole world just yet). We pick up a couple of skinny lattes and head back to The Globe, a large pub on the corner opposite Baker Street tube station. The place is quiet, so we help ourselves to their garden furniture and watch the traffic go by.

Not for the first time, it's hard to find the right words. It's over. We can draw our line right here, on the pavement outside The Globe public house if we want to. If I had a paintbrush I'd be tempted. The significance of the day is just beginning to sink in for both of us, when I see that Lesley is crying. Naturally, I'm doing that whole manly British thing and keeping a stiff upper lip. I'm being strong as usual and, if there's a shoulder to cry on around here, then it will be mine. It's a surprise then to feel tears rolling down my own cheeks.

Several gulps of coffee later and we have both regained

some of our earlier composure. We needed a moment of release of some kind, and that was obviously it. With the cloud lifted we can talk freely, and we start to imagine what our friends and family will have to say. They are full of well meaning ideas and always seem a lot less prepared to give up on our dreams than we are. Soon enough, they'll be asking us what our next steps are.

So what do we fancy trying next? Egg donation? Surrogacy? It won't be easy to tell them that we're finished with all that. *What about adoption?* That's a whole different ball game. No one could ever accuse us of not trying hard enough to have a child, but are we ready to take on someone else's? Right now, as we try to recover from the bruising we've taken over the last few years, I don't really think so.

No, it may come as a disappointment to some of the people we know, but we have an exciting future to look forward to – together. Just the two of us. And, with no snotty-nosed little kids to get in our way, we can plan that future and enjoy it. Any way we like. It's not where we expected to come out of all this, but we can make it work.

Wednesday 18 January 2006

They say the difference between men and boys is the price of their toys. I've worked out that without children our disposable income levels should hold up pretty nicely in the years to come, thank you very much, and I could get used to this kind of lifestyle. Oh, what toys we will have.

The bright colours of our new 37" flat screen plasma TV in the living room are enough to make your eyes water, while the Dolby Prologic amplifier and speaker system I've just finished hooking up could blow your brains out with an almighty burst of crystal clear surround sound.

I have actually lost count of the digital DAB radios and DVD players we now have in the house – but what's a room without a digital radio, or ready access to our growing movie library? I'm a sucker for gadgets and, would you believe it, they seem to be popping up everywhere these days.

We finally sorted out our money with the embryology clinic today too. *Five grand in your pocket, chum, and let's hear no more about it.* It's not compensation for anything. It's simply a business transaction – our money back, plus some incidental expenses. No more, no less, but a reasonable gesture nonetheless, and a welcome sum of cash. With it, we plan to book that holiday in Canada we've had our eye on for a while. A holiday is a very different kind of toy, I grant you, but I think it counts toward our total if anyone's actually keeping score.

Our lives have new rules now – we can spend our money however we want, do what we want, and we can drop everything whenever we want. We can go away for the weekend, go out for a meal, or just hang out with our friends (preferably the ones without any of those infernal young children). We're free from the awkward ties and commitments that blight the lives of so many people and stop them having all the fun they deserve.

Until recently, it's fair to say that neither Lesley nor I ever imagined this would be the way we'd want to live our lives, but right now it has a certain appeal. The chance to buy and own lots of new and exciting things is something most parents miss out on big time. They are too busy changing nappies and making ends meet. Where's the fun in any of that? We can count ourselves lucky that we didn't fall into that trap after all. And we came mighty close once or twice.

Our new outlook on life reminds me of those crazy days of the 1980s. When that madcap duo of Ronnie and Maggie struck up their special relationship to teach us all that "greed is good" and that the most important thing in life is to put yourself first. Beat thy neighbour and grab what you can was their advice – which was great if you were the one doing the grabbing, although it was pretty rough on the neighbours.

I didn't much care for any of that at the time, but I do remember a phrase that popped up on bumper stickers all over the USA, describing a new philosophy for this modern age that Thatcher and Reagan had worked so hard to create. I don't think anyone knows who actually came up with it, but it appears to define the one simple rule to follow if you are hoping to win the game of life.

"*The one who dies with the most toys wins.*"

Forget about the Ten Commandments and the "Seven Habits of Highly Effective People". Put away your Koran, your Bible and even your "Tao of Pooh". Don't worry about how you raise your kids, so long as you teach them that their main goal in life is to own a Porsche. It's not about the stuff you do any more, it's all about the stuff you *buy*. The 1980s are on their way back in our house and we know the golden rule. Lesley and I are agreed on the new philosophy round here.

It's OK that we can't have children.

We gave it our best shot, but these are the cards fate has dealt us. We can't have children, but there's no reason why we can't have the most toys.

17

Waiting

I have been in this place for such a long time I hardly notice the icy walls of the great hollow cavern around me any more. It has become normal to me here – it's where I live, it's where I wait. There used to be a million reasons to get out into the sunlight, but now...I just don't know. Life is simpler here in the dark and it's tempting to ignore the cracks in the ice when you've forgotten what it really was you wanted on the outside. But there is something out there, something that I need. Something that's missing from my life here, however hard I try to convince myself otherwise. I may have even glimpsed it through the cracks. I just need to gather up the courage to break free and go find it.

Sunday 15 July 2007

I never imagined the whole course of my life changing while walking down the frozen food aisle at Tesco, but I think that may have just happened.

There I was one moment, digging deep among the

packs of broccoli and sprouts, making sure that whatever frozen vegetables I could find hadn't been "exposed to the air". It's a long-standing habit I have when food shopping and Lesley ribs me mercilessly on the subject – even if it only ranks third behind my obsessive compulsion to buy things in even numbers and my still unabated need to fill our fridge with copious amounts of milk at every turn.

The next thing I knew I was casually asking my wife about a leaflet she had left on the coffee table in the living room, just a couple of days earlier.

'I picked it up at the doctor's surgery last week,' she told me, all matter of fact as we trundled our trolley towards the vast racks of Hovis on the shelves just ahead of us. 'It's from one of those agencies…you know…'

'…one of those adoption agencies.' I finished her sentence in my head before she could even speak the words.

'They're an adoption agency,' she confirmed, in a voice hushed almost to a whisper.

Of course I knew that already, but I didn't want to give the game away. I had read the leaflet as soon as I saw it. I'm sure that was what Lesley had intended.

'Oh?' I prompted.

'I thought we might look into it.'

'OK.'

And that was all it took – no in-depth discussion, no painful heart-to-heart. Just 'I thought we might look into it' and 'OK'. Thirty seconds ago we were free to spend our money however we wanted, do whatever we wanted whenever we wanted. It didn't always feel right, but I was getting used to it.

Suddenly, and seemingly out of nowhere, adoption is on our agenda and that could change everything. So what happened to 'not a chance'? That's what we've been telling everyone. I mean, didn't we rule all this out ages ago? We have tried so hard to build our own family and look what happened to us – and to Lesley in particular. I'm lucky to still have my wife at all and it's taken us a long time to come to terms with our "loss". Are we really prepared to take on *someone else's* children after all that?

Entranced by the seemingly endless rows of bread choices on the shelves in front of me, my mind drifts back three months and I realise how overdue the brief conversation we've just had really is.

Once again, we were on our travels – a child-free excursion to a beautiful resort in Malaysia this time. It was there that we met Gabby, a two-year old Chinese girl, completely adorable and happily playing with her white Australian parents. There was no need to ask whether Gabby was adopted, all you could see was a beautiful and happy family. Neither Lesley nor I could bring ourselves to put it into words even then, but we both knew we wanted to be in that picture and it brought a lump to the throat.

So are we really prepared to take on someone else's children after all that's happened? After all our big talk about life without kids and how that could work for us?

As I pick up a couple of loaves and chuck them rather casually into our trolley, I know the answer to my question is 'yes'. For both of us. Absolutely, positively and definitively yes. Deep down I know it always has been. Even if it has taken us a very long time to admit it and we couldn't actually speak the words until today.

Tuesday 17 July 2007

When I look around the room, there's a remarkable cross section of people here. There's the suited and booted, the slick, the casual and the ever so slightly *chavvy*...all the way to the downright oddball. I start to wonder where Lesley and I might fit into this eclectic mix and find myself hoping that we don't slot too readily into the latter category.

Actually, this place (a community centre not so far from home) is full of people just like us – we are all attending an introductory meeting for potential adopters run by two social workers from our local council's children's services team. It seems astonishing that '*I thought we might look into it*' has led us to this in the space of 48 hours, but Lesley has been busy. I had always thought the adoption process was a long and drawn-out one, yet it's zipping along for us already.

After looking through the "introduction to adoption" leaflet again on Sunday, we decided to do some research on local adoption agencies. There were a few options, but the most obvious seemed to be our local council. After all, they are the ones who actually have all the children waiting for adoption. And as this particular leg of our journey began in a supermarket, it seemed right to start with a one-stop-shop.

Lesley filled in a form on the council's website yesterday and was surprised when someone from their children's services team called her within the hour to suggest we attend today's meeting. These introductory sessions are only run every two or three months, so we had a choice – drop everything and get down here, or join the queue for the next one in September.

The meeting is led by an experienced social worker called Penny – she is absolutely compelling and manages to combine friendly with serious in a way that never puts you completely at ease. She has an almost hypnotic voice and, as she talks about what becoming an adopter is really like, it soon becomes obvious that she intends to scare the living daylights out of everyone in the room.

There is a hint of *Alcoholics Anonymous* about the meeting. We're all nervous, unsure what to expect, and I for one am finding it hard to resist the urge to stand up and announce that: 'My name's Mike Butcher and I'm a childless would-be parent!'

One look into Penny's eyes convinces me that this is neither the time nor the place for such flippancy. Adoption is no easy option and should not be entered into lightly. The social workers make that quite clear and I believe them.

The adoption process itself is clearly designed to weed out anyone who doesn't make the grade, or who isn't really up for the challenge. As Penny reels off many of the difficulties that can arise, the problems the children may have experienced, and the effect all of that can have on you as an individual or as a couple, I realise that this meeting is very much part of that "weeding out" process.

It's fair to say that, for Lesley and me, today is a wake up call. OK, so we may have both been secretly contemplating the notion of adopting for quite some time now. Certainly, us being here is not all down to an impulsive decision made under the mad consumerist influence of Tesco, but – as they say – '*every little helps*'.

Until now we haven't given much serious thought to the *reality* of adopting a child, and all the issues that come with it. Penny is doing her best to change that, as she runs through a very long list of events and stages we will have to go through if we decide adoption is for us. There is a lot to take in about the process itself, the time and patience you need, the intrusion into your life, the potential for disappointments and the desperate need for a dependable support network to help you survive everything that might come your way.

Then there are all those tricky questions you have to ask yourselves:

Can we give up our easy life and take all this on?

Are we strong enough to battle through the process?

What kind of problems could we really deal with?

What age of child or children are we looking for?

To be honest, we don't have the answers to these questions right now. There's so much for us to think about, although I do toy with offering '22 years old, with a job in the City and his or her own house' to the last question. Still cautious in the presence of two very nice but slightly intimidating social workers, I resist the urge to speak and keep my mouth firmly shut.

The meeting lasts for a couple of hours – we get to see a few short video clips and, at the end, we are even introduced to a real live adopter. This is encouraging, because after hearing how hard the whole thing is, it's a relief to hear from someone who has actually been through everything they've described today and lived to tell the tale.

She tells us how she and her husband adopted two boys. They were brothers and both quite young at the time, each bringing their own individual set of challenges and rewards. That was five years ago and, while she is honest enough to admit that neither the process nor the adoption itself were always a bed of roses, overall they have found the whole experience to be truly wonderful.

It's a great way to close the session and, if we're not quite bouncing with excitement at the end, we are geared up for the challenge and optimistic about our chances. With everything we have survived as a couple over the last few years, we are confident that we can cope with what's to come.

On our way out, we pick up an information pack and a magazine called *Be My Parent* – the adoption world's version of the Argos catalogue. It's full of smiling children desperately needing parents, and a quick flick through the pages is enough to make your heart melt. Lesley and I have a lot of talking to do when we get home, to try and put everything we have heard today into some kind of context. The truth is, we have absolutely no idea what we are getting into. We have spent the afternoon hearing that it will take forever for things to happen, and when they do, we may just regret it forever.

I have to admit, I'm still nervous and it's as scary as hell. *But it's fantastic!*

Neither of us has felt this excited in years. Oh yes, it will be tough. There'll be sacrifices. Lesley and I have a lot of questions to answer and there's much about the way we live that will probably have to change. But we'll make it fun – for us and any child or children who happen to walk into our lives. Just you see if we don't!

The next step is for us to send a form to the children's services team to confirm that we wish to proceed. They will then arrange a proper meeting with us both. If, after this, they consider us to be suitable prospective adopters, we will be asked to attend a "Preparation Group" – a four-day training course, which I suspect will be significantly more demanding than today's session was.

Only when we have successfully completed this training will we be assigned a social worker and start off on the adoption process proper with what is called the "Home Study" – a series of eight meetings, give or take a few, held over several months and designed to explore every nook and cranny of our personalities, backgrounds and lives.

Having come this far in just 48 hours, it is easy to get carried away and imagine that we are going to fly through this next bit in a couple of weeks. Who knows, perhaps we'll be welcomed into the full adoption process by the end of the week and be assigned our very own social worker before the month is out...

Yes, and our cat will probably be awarded the Nobel Peace Prize for his services to ornithology...

You'll have noticed that the years have done nothing to quell my vivid imagination and unfettered optimism, whatever obstacles we come up against. But from everything we've heard today, I'm guessing that this rapid pace of activity is something Lesley and I had better not get used to.

Tuesday 4 September 2007
We are under no illusions any more. Certainly not when it

comes to how long everything is likely to take and my foolish hope that we might be the couple in a million that bucked the trend and galloped through the whole adoption process in record time. We have heard nothing at all from the council since our meeting in July. In fact, things have gone so quiet that we have decided to look elsewhere while we are waiting. The adoption leaflet Lesley picked up was produced by what is known as a "voluntary agency", so we dug it out again and gave their number a call to ask what they could do for us.

Now I'm not sure if it's entirely ethical to play the field with adoption agencies, but we figured that there are not many really important things that you do without checking out the various options. This is one of the biggest decisions of our lives, so why not see what a voluntary agency has to offer? These organisations are registered charities, after all, and they have a reputation for moving things along at a considerably faster pace than your average council ever can.

We went along to an introductory session at the agency's offices within a few days of this initial contact and were surprised to find that almost the whole meeting was handed over to one of their adopters to talk us through the adoption process. To be fair, he was great and did a terrific job of illustrating the highs and lows, and in outlining what we might have to look forward to. But it did seem an awful lot of responsibility to thrust onto his shoulders.

The most encouraging thing for Lesley and me that day was how much more confident about everything we felt already. The introductory session with our local children's services team, the magazines we'd looked at and the books we'd read had all given us a much clearer picture. At the end of the voluntary agency's session we were happy to put our names forward for the next stage and they were quick to offer us a follow-up meeting.

Arriving at the agency's office again today, we don't

know what to expect. It's like turning up for a job interview, but a whole lot more important. We sit down with one of their newest social worker recruits and she starts firing off all sorts of questions about our lives, what brings us here, our family backgrounds and even our finances.

Many of the questions are open-ended, like 'tell me about your childhood', and we are unsure exactly what she is looking for. Is the answer (a) 'it was that bit of my life when I wasn't an adult', or is it (b) 'a time when Father Christmas still existed'? Perhaps she wants us to tell her how we were both beaten regularly and locked in the shoe cupboard for hours on end? Or how we were signed up by our parents to become chimney sweeps at the age of seven?

We have no such horrors to report, so we look to the social worker for some guidance – some further explanation of what they are getting at. But she keeps asking the questions. By the end of the session, we are not really feeling positive at all. We are not upset with the poor woman asking us the questions – she is just doing her job. And it's not that we feel challenged by what has happened, or how the meeting went. It actually seemed to go all right. We just feel confused.

Everything about the notion of adopting has felt right up until now. Even the waiting around has given us time to think. We just want to get on with it now and see some progress. And that's exactly what the team at the voluntary agency appear to be offering us. Assuming they will have us at all, of course. This is something we will find out only after the social worker has written up her notes from our meeting and spoken to her manager. Her green light could lead to us attending their next Preparation Group in October, with the realistic prospect of racing through the whole Home Study by the end of April next year.

The timing is oh-so-tempting, but for the first time since our "Tesco moment" back in July, there's a doubt gnawing at our resolve. Driving home from the meeting this afternoon, Lesley and I are of one mind. This doesn't feel right at all.

18

Be prepared

However hard you try, there are some things in life no one can ever really prepare you for. Bungee jumping comes to mind (never going to happen), walking on the moon (unlikely) or having a child (chance would be a fine thing!) It doesn't stop people trying though, and you soon become accustomed to the lectures on how long to make the bungee rope, what kind of spacesuits the most fashionable astronauts around town are wearing these days, and – well, let's be honest – the whole "child in your life" thing is a heap more difficult than any of that. My head is spinning, but at least I'm not short of advice.

Thursday 20 September 2007

Without warning, the pace started to pick up a bit the week after our meeting with the voluntary agency. First, a very official letter dropped through our door with a local postmark. It could only have come from the council. My first thought was that they had got wind of our recent meeting and were writing to chastise us for this blatant display of disloyalty.

Actually the children's services team had finally got round to offering us a follow-up meeting. At last! Their letter contained no apology for the long wait, or any kind of explanation for the delay. It seems these timescales are "business as usual" in the council's world and we had better get used to them if we want to go their way, rather than taking the voluntary agency's short cut.

Adding to this virtual whirlwind of activity, the agency social worker telephoned us a couple of days later to confirm that her manager had agreed to take us on as prospective adopters. If we were happy to proceed with them, she could book us on their Preparation Group in October.

Suddenly, from nothing happening at all, it was decision time.

Well, almost. I've still not seen anything in the adoption books that suggests you can't hedge your bets – just a little. We explained that we needed some time to think it over and, in the meantime, went ahead and scheduled today's visit from the council's social workers. While this did feel a teensy bit sneaky, it was nice to have a sense of control for the first (and probably last) time on the road to adoption.

Waiting for Ann and Beth this afternoon, I am already feeling less in control – although I am still more relaxed about this meeting than I expected. It certainly helps that they are coming to our house. It is obviously more convenient, not having to traipse across the county to some nondescript office, and enjoying "home advantage" on a day like this is a welcome factor.

Having experienced a similar meeting a couple of weeks back is a bit of a mixed blessing. We didn't much enjoy that encounter, and essentially we will be covering much the same ground today. But it does feel quite different here at home, even before we get started.

When the two social workers arrive, they are like a

breath of fresh air and our last dregs of anxiety evaporate quickly. They immediately put us at our ease and settle themselves down in our living room. Ann is our main contact and will lead the meeting, while Beth is here to support and make notes. As expected, we cover all those childhood questions; how long Lesley and I have been together; our history of infertility; and much more. But at no point do we feel adrift.

Ann is masterful at prompting us when we get stuck. It turns out that Beth, who has warned us she will be fairly quiet throughout the meeting, is far too enthusiastic a character to be anything of the sort, and so she chips in regularly.

It's a bit like being on the psychiatrist's couch (but in a good way – I think). They get to hear about my dad and the funny stories he used to make up for my brothers and me when we were kids. Lesley talks about her mum, the victim of breast cancer at the cruelly young age of 61. The inevitable tale of woe that took us on an unscheduled detour to Hammersmith comes up too.

She's a quiet one, that Ann, but she knows how to get at the information she needs and Beth's notebook is full by the time they finish the "interview". Finally, they take a whistle stop tour of our house before rushing off to their next appointment.

Once they have left, I turn to Lesley and I can see what she is thinking. This is another of those line drawing moments that have come up in our lives from time to time and it feels like a massive weight has been lifted off our shoulders. A big hug confirms it – that was a terrific meeting. It couldn't have gone any better. Ann and Beth have been warm, friendly, reassuring and – above all – what they don't know about adoption, about the "children who wait" and about prospective adoptive parents like us... well, it just isn't worth knowing.

We know the social workers at the voluntary agency are

likely to whisk us through the whole process much quicker than the council team could ever hope to. We know that with the council, we'll be waiting well into the New Year even to get on to a Preparation Group, let alone start with our Home Study. We know that with the council, all the waiting will be as frustrating as it gets. But after today, there is only one way for us to go.

Saturday 1 December 2007

Did I happen to mention that when you are thinking of adopting, all the waiting is as frustrating as it gets? I wasn't kidding. Actually, it's not so much the waiting… it's the not knowing how long you will have to wait that really frustrates you.

After our fateful decision to reject the voluntary agency in favour of our local authority, things went very quiet for ages. Not that we in any way regretted our decision, but we were conscious that things were stalling again and we still had a long way to go.

Finally, in mid-November, Lesley spoke to Beth and we organised a short catch-up meeting with her at her office. It turned out there had been some kind of communications mix-up between us – a letter had clearly gone astray somewhere. Beth was just as concerned that we hadn't been in touch with her or Ann for a while, thinking that we had maybe changed our minds about the whole thing.

On the positive side, it was good to hear that they obviously didn't want to lose us. On the negative, Beth still didn't really have any firm news for us on the Preparation Group, but she was trying very hard to get us on the next one due to start at the end of February.

Yes, February – that's close to three months away. I think I mentioned at some point that the waiting is just a little bit frustrating…

In the meantime, all we can do is get on with it and try to prepare ourselves for what we are letting ourselves in for here. We have been spending time with people we know who have already adopted, we are making more time for the children of our family and friends, and Lesley has even signed up as a Brownie leader with a local pack. The very thought of doing such a thing would send shivers down the spines of most people, but my wife loves it to bits.

The girls have given her a Brownie name, in the spirit of Brown Owl and the like. Lesley is known as Blackbird, which is lucky for me, as that is one of only three species of bird that I would ever admit to recognising. In my world, if it's not a budgie or a chicken, then it must be a blackbird. I have similar rules when it comes to the names of flowers and breeds of dog. It takes all the unnecessary complexity out of the natural world and leaves me room in my brain to store lots of far more important nonsense that is bound to come in useful one day.

Lesley and I have also both volunteered to help at our local Child Contact Centre. The commitment is minimal and is confined to just one Saturday a month, but it's like stepping through a gateway into a world I have never given any thought to before. More *Harry Potter* than *Narnia*, the Contact Centre is basically a place where a non-resident parent can go to spend time with their child in a safe environment.

Today is my first full morning here and I'm nervous. The venue is an old Methodist Church and, if alcohol weren't taboo here, I could easily convince myself that we were running a prohibition era *Speakeasy*. On arrival, you have to ring the dedicated Contact Centre bell on the outside wall, alerting someone upstairs to your presence so that they can come down to let you in. It is far from intentional, but this creates an element of shiftiness, whether you are the gatekeeper or the poor soul seeking entry to this mysterious new world.

The fact is that this could be a very sad place, supporting families that have been broken up for all manner of reasons. The surprising thing is that, on the whole, it isn't a sad place at all. Actually, there is an addictive and upbeat quality about my first full session at the Child Contact Centre. Even after a couple of hours I can see that we are offering an invaluable service.

And it really doesn't matter if it's hard or awkward (or even downright embarrassing) for either parent to be here, it is terrific that the children have this opportunity to maintain some kind of meaningful relationship with their non-resident mum or dad. It would be easy to take sides or to be swayed by the emotional intensity of the various situations we see unfolding in front of our eyes, but that is not what we are here to do as volunteers. And if, as the novice around here, I ever look likely to fall into this or any other trap, then help is close to hand.

We have an inspirational leader in Maureen Randall, a retired social worker and manager of our disparate band of Contact Centre helpers. If I needed a role model when it comes to understanding or dealing with children in testing circumstances (and I probably will), then I couldn't possibly go far wrong with Maureen as a mentor. She is a diminutive dynamo with a sparkle in her eyes that I know I can relate to. Importantly, Maureen is sensitive to the adults' needs around here, but she never – and I mean *never* – puts their concerns above those of the children.

My morning flies by at the Contact Centre, despite any trepidation I might have had beforehand. The session has exceeded my expectations and I can really see how this kind of experience will help me build my confidence around children and prepare me for what Lesley and I might have to confront.

Maybe I haven't quite believed it up to this point, but today has confirmed one thing for me. (And it's a biggie.) This is really happening. We are serious about adopting. Even if I wanted to, I don't think there is anything I could do to stop it now.

Friday 29 February 2008

We have trodden a long and winding road just to get to this point, but at four o'clock this afternoon we completed day two of our Preparation Group. We're still knocking on the door of the business end of the adoption process, but we are well aware that this four-day training course is a major hurdle for us to clear.

It's been all of seven months since our first contact with the council, so I count it as a bonus that we have an extra day to play with this year. Every day counts and today has definitely been my most memorable – February 29th, the eleventh "leap day" of my life, if I have my sums right. It's been the most emotional too. They don't pull many punches on these adoption-training courses. We've been asked to look very deeply into ourselves these past couple of days. To think about who we are, what makes us who we are, and the problems we have overcome, or have yet to overcome.

We've also discussed children, how they establish their identity, their resilience, what affects their development and the problems this may cause at a young age, throughout their school and teenage years, and even as adults.

We've seen a case study about a child with cerebral palsy, rejected by both parents and neglected for the first two years of her life. We have had to consider our reaction to a seven-year-old boy whose regular exposure to violence, whether on TV or in the home, leads him to chasing his adoptive cousin out into the garden, locking her in a Wendy House and terrorising her with a sharp stick.

There was something about this last scenario that raised uncomfortable smiles and a few nervous chuckles among the group, but our reactions were noticeably defensive. The situation described wasn't funny; it conjured up a bizarre image that was just so awful, none of us could even begin to imagine how we would deal with it. Although we were all agreed – the sharp stick would have to go.

Our "preparation" is a shared experience and we are part of a group of 17 attending this course, packed into a room only just about big enough to squeeze us all in. Then there are the three social workers: Lesley and Debra who are running the course and one more, our old friend Penny, rather ominously there to observe and make notes.

We have joined the group to learn, but it is made clear that we will be subject to scrutiny throughout the four days. Certainly everything about the sessions has been set up to make them open and non-threatening, but the presence of an observer is a little unnerving and I wonder to what extent that is affecting or inhibiting the group's behaviour. So far, I think I've done an OK job of keeping my natural irreverence and fondness for inappropriate *non-sequiturs* in check, but goodness knows if I can keep it up for four days.

Still, it's been great to meet so many people going through the same process we are, and all having arrived at the same point. We are a mixed bunch, so it has been enlightening to talk to the others about how they reached this stage and why they have decided, as we have, that adoption is for them. Some of the group have been down the IVF road like Lesley and me, while others already have birth children and have chosen adoption to build their families further. Gluttons for punishment, I can't help thinking, but there you are, and talking with them helps us to understand their personal motivations.

One of these couples already has considerable experience as foster carers and they have brought a quite different slant to the discussions, along with bags of knowledge that the rest of us feel the need to catch up with.

Before we started the Preparation Group yesterday, the whole notion of training to be adopters seemed an odd one. Many of our friends have been shocked and even outraged when they found out that we have to do this – offended on our behalf that anyone could dare suggest it might be necessary. Two days in, and I would say that it is.

Whether we will actually learn much during the course I don't know, but the Preparation Group is much more than that. It's about arranging all those jumbled thoughts you might have about adoption into the right order. It's about seeing the world from the child's perspective. And it's about testing yourself.

If you can't hack a four-day course like this one, then you might as well pack up and go home. Or at least re-evaluate where you really are. Adoption is a lifelong commitment and, after these last couple of days, Lesley and I are more certain than ever that we are in it for the long haul.

Friday 23 May 2008

It is seven years to the day since Lesley was rushed off to Queen Charlotte's hospital in Hammersmith. Seven years since I took part in that mad dash behind an ambulance that, as it turned out, had no idea where it was actually going. Seven years during which, if we're honest, neither Lesley nor I have really known where we were going either.

Today all that has changed.

23rd May is not a date I would normally mark on the calendar, but today Ann called to say we have been cleared to begin our Home Study with an allocated member of their team. All along, she has stressed that the social worker chosen to take us through this final process can't be someone we know well, or be someone who has been heavily involved with us before. That rules out all three of the social workers who participated in our Preparation Group. It also rules out Ann and Beth.

A couple of weeks after our training had finished in March we were called in to the office to discuss how we'd handled it. This was "make or break" time. A green light here would see us proceed further, while a critical assessment could set us back months, or even derail our efforts altogether. To our relief, they seemed to like us. We actually met up with Ann and Penny, who had been so busily scribing for four days as the observers on our course. They ran through their impressions of us and their interpretation of our attitude to the training – how far we had come and the areas they were keen for us to work on or try to add further to our experience.

We really didn't do badly at all and everything sounded jolly promising – although where they got the idea that my occasional and most uncharacteristic random use of humour might be a source of concern if directed towards a child (or worse still, a social worker), I will never know!

Not long after this meeting, we were invited to a group session to discuss adoption with three local adopters. The evening was an encouraging one for us and many of our fellow trainees, and it seemed to signal a significant change of tactics on the part of the social workers. Despite all the obvious downsides, the people we met that night actually seemed to think adoption was a good idea and were keen to share the positive stuff.

The only slightly cautionary note came from a woman who had adopted a five-year-old boy two or three years ago. She was surprised by the way he confidently called her Mum within minutes of meeting her and was happy to talk about his "forever family". When she challenged the young lad about what being his "forever Mum" actually meant, he thought about it for a moment before replying. 'When you die, I'll get your house!' he told her, as matter of fact as you like.

It was hard to imagine being on her side of that particular conversation – but looking on the bright side, if things could work out for her family after a beginning like that, then adoption has to be a good thing after all.

And today we have been allocated a social worker.

That means we are in. We have come through and this whole thing is going ahead. We *will* get through the Home Study, we *will* be going to an "Adoption Panel" – where their job is to recommend to the authority whether we should be approved as adopters – and, barring the revelation that we have been war criminals in a previous life or something like that, we *will* have the chance to adopt a child.

Wow!

Seven long years since all our plans began unravelling big time and we've finally made it. We have a new plan now and, while we are under no illusions about the hard work yet to come, this is a big moment for us. We have been wondering for a while whom they might allocate to us and whether we will be happy with the choice. We needn't have worried. As it turns out, we have Ann after all. I guess pressures of work in the team have over-ridden other factors. Ann is our allocated social worker and we couldn't be more delighted to get started with her.

I realise now that 10 years or more of trying to build a family have brought us inevitably to this moment. The ups and the downs, the pain and frustration, and a whole set of emotions that have been far more mixed than Lesley or I could ever have anticipated. They have all contributed to us reaching this point.

I am as certain as I can be now that we *will* be parents. Maybe not in quite the way we had imagined, but it could even be better this way. Somehow even more special than we had ever dreamed possible.

19

Unfrozen

It is around 23 degrees Celsius outside today. It's been a long time since Lesley and I have felt warm at all, but I think we could get used to this. We're thrilled with thoughts that we sometimes find hard to comprehend and we're caught up in a burst of activity that might draw us out into the sunshine for good. Neither of us expected to feel this way, but we do. Truth is, things have taken a pretty weird turn, but it's not that. Weird we could always handle – we've had enough practice. No, there's something else and right now we have no idea where it may lead. Or how long it will take us to get there. All we do know is that it promises to be the most amazing journey of our lives.

Friday 24 October 2008

The last time I remember getting into such a detailed discussion about family history was with my grandfather 30 years ago. He regaled my brothers and me with grand tales of smugglers off the Kent coast and German immigrants fleeing Napoleonic invaders. They were all strands of the family story, as recalled by his own grandfather when he was a little boy – though I should point out that my grandfather was a masterful storyteller, so he may have embellished the stories just a little.

Whatever the truth about the illicit rum dealers and political asylum seekers in the Butchers' murky past, I realised quite some time ago that this is more information than Ann really needs for our Home Study report, so I stick to more contemporary details for my family tree.

Of course, our family history is just one among many things that Ann requires to paint a fully rounded picture of Lesley and me as potential adopters. She needs our height, weight, a current photograph, full details of our support network, no less than eight personal referee statements between us (at least three of which will require face-to-face interviews), and our educational histories, inside leg measurements and shoe sizes. All right, so I made the last two up, but you get the picture – and that's just skimming the surface of the dossier we are aiming to compile.

I have even been forced to divulge my criminal past. Well, "criminal" may be putting it a bit strongly, but you are asked to declare any convictions you may have on the appropriate page of the potential adopters form and I can't deny an event that goes all the way back to my student days at the University of York.

It was early 1986 – my last year of full-time education – and I was mounting the ramparts of the establishment in one final flush of rebellion against the Government's plans to cut student grants. There were about 200 of us on that march through the streets of York, all ready to take on the authorities with our slogans and placards. I could hear Maggie Thatcher quaking in her boots somewhere in far off Downing Street.

Those were tense days, however, and, with the ill-fated Miners' Strike of '84–85 still fresh in everyone's minds, the police were somewhat tetchy. They soon made it clear that they didn't want us to march at all and rather foolishly, I can now reflect, around 50 of us promptly decided to blockade the street instead by plonking our bums down on the road.

Before I knew it, I was being bundled into the back of a police van by two burly officers along with 20 other protestors who, like me, had failed to run away at an opportune moment. I wound up spending several hours in a small cell with a couple of confused anarchists and half a dozen emotional members of the Socialist Workers Party, all rather worried about how Ma and Pa back home on the country estate might view their brush with the law.

I copped a £50 fine for "obstructing the public highway" that day (a civil rather than a criminal offence, I hasten to point out for any social workers or prospective employers reading this book), but I knew it would all be worth it in the end. After all, how could any right-minded government ignore such an act of revolutionary heroism?

As it happens, my defence of student liberty (and beer money) was so spectacularly unsuccessful that grants were phased out altogether over the next few years. Then, when the people of Britain finally elected a Labour government in 1997, the new administration casually leapt in and introduced tuition fees for students on top of everything else.

Thank you so much, Mr Blair – can I have my 50 quid back?

Strangely, Ann doesn't include all of this detail on our Home Study form, but we are getting there. In fact, this part of the process has proved to be nowhere near as tough as we thought it would be. It takes a long time, but we are open people. Ann is not having much trouble at all in prising what she needs from us and the meetings are regular enough to fool us into thinking things are moving along quite fast.

The only hitch now is that Lesley has rashly gone and

injured her ankle while hiking in Devon back in June. She struggled along with the pain for almost three months, but a proper assessment has determined that the injury requires surgery to repair all the damaged ligaments and tendons. We have been told that our Adoption Panel, provisionally scheduled for mid-December, will probably need to be postponed.

It seems that Lesley will have to undergo the operation and make a full recovery before they will entertain us as prospective adopters – and, as that could take 10–12 weeks, a new date in January already looks our best bet. Ann was very apologetic when she gave us the news, but she has assured us it will be for the best. Lesley really wouldn't want to attend the Panel on crutches, she keeps telling us, and what's another month or so after all this time?

While this is a development we weren't really anticipating, Lesley and I are quite accustomed to setbacks by now. Delays come with the territory in the adoption business. And we can't fail to notice a peculiar symmetry to events as I take Lesley in for her operation today.

Here we are again…

At the same local private hospital. Where we had all that fertility treatment. Where our journey really began. Who would have thought we would be back here? At a time like this? Sometimes the mind boggles and the whole world seems to join in.

Friday 20 February 2009

I am wearing my best suit, Lesley is in a smart grey outfit bought especially for the day. The only crutch we have with us today is Ann, who will support us in our Adoption Panel meeting at 10.45 this morning.

We are finally here. Decision day. Well, almost: the Panel will recommend; the agency (the council) will decide. So what if January turned into February, I'm not complaining. From what I hear, everyone gets bumped off at least one of these panels – they are very busy affairs and their available slots fill up very fast. I'm happy now that Lesley's ankle has healed nicely and our day at County Hall has arrived at last.

Ann shows us to a waiting room where she explains that tea and coffee have been laid on for us. We actually find two big flasks filled with hot water and a supply of Nescafé sachets and Tetley tea bags. She heads off to the Panel meeting room while we look around for the fine china, or at least a paper cup or two. Nothing doing – but there are four moulded plastic cups that unscrew from the top of the flasks…

It feels like we are taking time out for a little picnic in a drab room in the middle of a large municipal building on the most important day of our lives. I help myself to a cup of slightly lukewarm tea anyway and, despite a brief attempt to sit down and patiently await our fate, we soon find ourselves pacing nervously around the table.

The wait is no more than half an hour, but it feels like forever. The way these things work is that the Panel members have all of the written reports up front and then spend some time discussing the merits or otherwise of the potential adopters who have come to see them. In our case, Ann has been on hand throughout this discussion to answer any questions about the report she has compiled. It is only when they are finished with all this that we are called in to face the music.

Walking into the room, we are confronted by no less than 17 people, all sitting around a horseshoe-shaped table arrangement. Uneasily I calculate that even murderers have fewer people sitting in judgment on them. There's a senior social worker, a local councillor, an adopter, an adopted person, a local magistrate, a doctor and several more. This could be very intimidating and I detect a frisson of nerves building up in Lesley to accompany the butterflies in my own stomach.

It helps that the members of our super-sized jury are so welcoming and so friendly, and I soon find myself enjoying the experience. They ask a few questions we were expecting and a couple we weren't, but we do our best to answer them all and hope that we can live up to their expectations. I even manage to weave an inappropriate gag into the proceedings, despite promising Lesley and Ann that I wouldn't. It's that tired old chestnut about the advantages of "buy one get one free" deals when they ask us why we have said we are happy to consider either one or two children if it is right for us and right for him, her or both of them.

The quip elicits a noticeable wince from Ann and a slight gasp from Lesley, but – thank goodness – a hearty ripple of laughter around the room. They are humans after all!

When they're done with us, Ann leads the way into an adjoining room where all three of us stand almost silently, hardly daring to breathe, and await the Panel's verdict. It's only two or three minutes – albeit a very long two or three minutes – before the Panel chair greets us with a big smile and the news we have been waiting for.

'We are delighted to recommend your approval,' she tells us.

There are hugs all round and, as we emerge from County Hall, it feels as though we are stepping free of those many years of heartbreak. Like the February sunshine that has so kindly seen fit to grace the occasion, our future seems bright. I look at Lesley and, as we both wipe away the tears – happy tears for once – we know that we are ready for what comes next.

But first we have to climb the hill.

Now, you might think the hill is yet another clumsy metaphor I've dreamed up to describe the matching process: the final stage of the mountain we have ascended over the past 18 months perhaps? But no. The hill is a real hill. Not a very big one, I'll concede, but it's a fantastic vantage point on a popular walking route just a few miles from home.

It's more than 10 years since we were first up there, standing at the top of the hill with an inspirational view across the local reservoirs and the green fields in the valley beyond. We were still getting started with all our fertility treatment back then, but we knew right away that when we were "pregnant", we would come back here and drink a small glass of champagne to celebrate.

We had set aside a very special bottle of sparkling plonk – actually it was nothing better than one of a pair of Lanson Black Labels we really did pick up on a "buy one get one free" offer at Threshers many years ago – and laid it down for a special day we had long thought would never come. That day is today and, while we may not technically be pregnant, this is definitely the next best thing.

The bottle is pretty dusty when we pick it off the wine rack and put it on ice, ready for our historic climb. In truth, it doesn't look as if it has kept well, but we are committed and the ritual is set for this afternoon. We have promised this to ourselves for far too long to back out now.

Once we're there, it doesn't take long for us to trot up the path to the highest point and crack open the champagne. The sun is still shining, which is a real bonus, but the wind is fierce. We chink our glasses and glug their contents between chattering teeth. It's not quite the idyllic scene I had always envisioned: we are pretty cold and the wine really doesn't taste that good. But the moment does.

Wednesday 3 June 2009

If anyone ever asks you what the hardest part of the adoption process is, you can tell them it's this bit. Tell them from me. The bit after all the preparation you have to do to get started in the first place, after all the hard work you need to put into completing the Home Study. The bit after all the euphoria of actually being approved to adopt a child.

The matching process – I am beginning to understand

that this is what they've really been preparing us for all this time. It's difficult, it's emotional and it feels like it's never going to end. It's only in the past three months that we have come to realise the true frustrations you face when trying to leap these final adoption hurdles. At this business end of proceedings, it's all or nothing, all the time.

Every day that passes, we are desperate to hear about another lead, another child who may become part of our lives forever. And, believe it or not, we've been lucky. There have been leads – several of them. Ann has mentioned three or four possibilities and we have even attended an Adoption Exchange day run by a consortium of local authorities, where you swap flyers advertising yourselves with details of children looking for a family.

We've been busy at home too. We have had a lot of work to contend with, terra-forming the house to accommodate the new life forms that may soon arrive and colonise the place. Of course, we still don't know whether we are talking about a boy or a girl, or one or two children. Crucially, we have no idea what age they will be either, as we are approved for the age group 0–5 years.

So we are doing what we can with the bedrooms and elsewhere, but there's a lot of beige paint and neutral decoration involved. Some of the more specific preparations will have to wait until the last minute, whenever that may be.

Talking to other potential adopters over the last few weeks has been something of a reality check though. A few of these couples have been waiting to be matched for over a year already and they are beginning to give up hope. Considering that there are so many children out there looking for families, this apparent inability to bring them together with people like us seems incomprehensible, but nothing in the adoption world is ever quite as straightforward as it seems.

It's not as if we have been short of possible matches.

Unfortunately, each time we have heard about one, something has come up that rules them out for us. Or we have hesitated, or things have gone very quiet while political (and financial?) calculations are made in the background as part of some inter-agency negotiation.

Ann has now come to the conclusion that we probably can't be matched to any of the children currently being looked after by our local children's services team due to "geographic" issues. It seems that we live too close to all of the children's families. But in the past few days we have had a couple more children scrubbed off our radar because their social workers wanted to place them closer to their current home, so we can't help but feel a little bit frustrated.

We have a holiday planned this month – one last hurrah before other things take precedence. A trip to Mauritius and a chance to chill out, I hope. I have proposed that we take a short break, forget about the matching and all the disappointments. We need to focus on ourselves and on our holiday – all this will still be here when we get back.

Lesley was almost convinced by my plan until Ann threw a brand new spanner into the works this morning. My wife was on her way to survey an office building some 50 miles from home when she took a call on her hands-free.

'I have some news,' Ann skipped the usual pleasantries and got straight to the point. 'Pull up somewhere, we need to talk.'

'I can't,' Lesley shrugged, 'I'm on the motorway.'

'You have to – call me back as soon as you can.'

With that she was gone. Suitably intrigued, Lesley pulled into the next services and dialled Ann's number...

A few minutes later Lesley is on the phone to me with an update. It seems that a social worker from one of the neighbouring counties has been in touch with Beth to ask about us.

'They want the Butchers,' Beth has told Ann.

'They want you,' Ann has told Lesley.

'Apparently they want us,' Lesley tells me rather excitedly.

But what exactly do they want us for? That's what I want to know. Apologies to everyone for my undisguised cynicism here, but after all those frustrating verses of the adoption Hokey Cokey we've put up with – well, I've had enough of this dancing around for the time being and I just want to go on holiday.

'We can talk about it later,' Lesley concedes, leaving me to scowl at my colleagues for the rest of the afternoon and to grumble under my breath about all my fellow commuters on the train home.

Lesley doesn't say a word when I walk through our front door tonight. She simply hands me a piece of paper she has collected in person from the children's services office this afternoon. I look down and realise I have a flyer in my hands with a picture and a short description of a beautiful baby boy. My heart skips several beats. He's just four months old and he's perfect.

'And Beth said...she really said...they want the Butchers?' I manage. 'They really want us?'

'Apparently so,' Lesley confirms.

Monday 6 July 2009

We should hear the all-important verdict today. I've even come home early from work because I want to be with Lesley when Ann calls us.

When you are considered as potential adopters for a child the norm is to shortlist two couples, both of which have to be a pretty good match or they wouldn't be in the frame. But the answer is always going to be 'yes' or 'yes, but' – which means 'no'. Either your life is about to change forever, or nothing happens at all.

Living on a knife's edge like this is not my idea of fun and I've probably been at my grumpiest best as the tension has grown since that initial approach 33 days ago. Anyone would think I've been counting.

Of course, we soon realised that "wanting the Butchers" and "wanting to interview the Butchers" are two different things, but they certainly had us interested. Our holiday suddenly seemed ill-timed, especially if it meant we'd have to wait until we got back to meet with the little boy's social workers. We offered to cancel the trip, but they told us not to worry. They could wait for us.

I had hoped that we could get away from it all for two weeks in Mauritius, relax and forget the stresses and the strains of the matching process. Not a chance. Everywhere we looked around our hotel we saw young toddlers with their parents and heavily pregnant mums-to-be. It's that time of year and it was that kind of hotel. We dared hope that it was a good omen, but barely a minute passed without us thinking about the meeting we would have when we came home.

The day of the meeting finally arrived – 24 June at 2.30pm (it's etched in my memory now). And, as anyone who has had one of these matching interviews knows, it is absolutely impossible to judge whether you have been successful or not. At job interviews you usually get a sense, an inkling of what they think of you, whether they want you. Matching interviews are nothing like that – the interviewers are too well trained and they give nothing away.

What's worse, our interviewers told us that we would have to wait 10 days or more for the verdict, as they still had to interview the other couple. All this waiting reminds me of those agonising days following our early adventures with IUI and IVF close to a decade ago now and even our final throw of the fertility dice in 2005. All we needed back then was one bit of luck, the right answer to that million-dollar question.

It never came and in a strange way now I'm glad. Despite everything, I like where we are right now. It's been tough, but it's been the most life-affirming *Mission Impossible* you could ever imagine. And if we could just get that one little bit of luck right now...

Finally, the phone rings and I watch my wife as Ann delivers the news. Then Lesley turns towards me, her face sculpted with the cheesiest grin I've ever seen.

'They chose us!' she beams.

Thursday 10 September 2009

There are days of your life you will never forget. I may have had more than my fair share already, but 2 September 2009 is out in front for me now. That's the day we met our son.

Following the decision to place him with us, there has been all the usual red tape to deal with: meetings with the medical adviser and his current foster carers; a placement planning meeting; more forms to fill in for the Panel that will be asked to recommend the match; and of course attending the Panel itself.

It has all taken time, but everything has gone without a hitch. After the Matching Panel, we agreed the final details of our "introductions" plan – the eight-day period that would bridge our first meeting with our child and the day our beautiful baby boy would join our family. And if that first meeting was special, it is hard to put into words what today means to us both. Today we get to take him home and we become Mum and Dad at last. It's a wonderful if daunting prospect.

During the introductions we have spent hours at the foster carers' house with our little boy. They have even brought him over to our house on a couple of days and he has spent quite a bit of time with us in his new home. It's all about making the transition as painless and natural as possible for all of us. And that includes his foster carers and the rest of their family, who must all be going through seven shades of hell at the prospect of losing him so soon.

Which will be in about an hour or so, I reckon, as this is all it will take us to drive to their house and pick him up.

We arrive at the foster carers' house and everything happens very fast. There are tears on all sides. Even the social workers present are struggling to contain their emotions. For almost the first time in my life I turn down the offer of a cup of tea. This has to be done quickly, for everyone's sake, and before we know it the most precious cargo we have ever carried is loaded into the car and we are on our way.

I pull off their drive and if I have ever driven more slowly and more carefully, I don't remember the time.

The road stretches out in front of us as we head home with our little boy safely on board. It's a couple of minutes before I realise I am holding my breath. I let out a big sigh and think of all the test tubes, the frozen embryos and the doctors; all the meetings, the forms and the social workers. The ups and the downs this journey has taken us on.

Suddenly none of that matters any more – we have the most amazing son and it's the best feeling ever.

I sneak a look at the little chap when we pull up at a traffic light. He has nodded off and gurgles lightly in his sleep. We still have a few more social worker visits to get through, a couple of formal reviews to attend and the legal adoption to complete the deal. Then there are all the joys and the heartaches our new lives will bring.

Everything that's gone and everything that's still to come – I know it's all been (and will be!) worth it. The proof of that is in the back of the car today. And, whatever the future holds for all three of us, we are a family now and we don't feel cold any more.

The beginning.

Final words

We really are very lucky. I can say that now. There were lots of times over the past 16 years when I didn't think that at all. When the whole idea of starting a family (as long ago as 1994) turned out to be not nearly as easy as we hoped it would be; when I was lying in that hospital bed back in 2001; when some of our embryos failed to show up in 2005; and even when we were grinding our way through the seemingly unending adoption process in 2008.

But we really are very lucky. Mike thinks that we must have been collecting little lumps of good fortune in exchange for some bad luck along our way, so that one day we could trade them all in for the one giant stroke of luck that might make it all worthwhile. As he puts it, 'the right answer to that million dollar question'. Mike's full of stuff like that, but this time I have to admit he may have a point. We have finally had that million dollar question answered – by a judge, no less. It doesn't get more official than that and I still have to pinch my arm on a regular basis to reassure myself that I am not dreaming.

We have now had all the meetings, we've been to the court, and we even have the relevant paperwork – including a lovely adoption certificate with coloured balloons on it. But best of all, we have a son. A beautiful, bright and amazing son. Our dreams have come true and we couldn't have hoped for a more wonderful outcome following many years of sadness and disappointment.

So why am I telling you all this? Because I want to share some of the happiness I am feeling right now? Maybe that's a part of it. But most of all, I want to express how lucky and happy I feel and try to explain how I got this way – in my own words.

A lot of people go through experiences like I did, especially when fertility treatment seems like their only option if they want to start a family. Not so many of them end up in intensive care of course, but there are worse things. When you spend years having your hopes dashed over and over again it does something to you as an individual and it does something to your relationship with your partner. Some couples don't survive it, so here's my first reason for my being so happy today – everything that happened to Mike and me made us stronger.

The hurt and disappointment took its toll on us all the same, even if I didn't exactly realise it at the time. It left a gaping hole in my life that I did my best to ignore for a very long while. And when your focus is on denying something like that to yourself, making the decision to look into another option is not an easy one. Looking back, I can honestly say that when I told people adoption wasn't for me, I really meant it.

The truth is, I had to recognise that gaping hole and make a decision to fill it before we could seriously consider adoption. My second reason for being so happy today is that by the time I was ready, Mike felt exactly the same. For so long our story seemed to be about failed fertility treatment and medical mix-ups, it seems strange now to acknowledge that the real problem was probably in both our heads. It's not that we were on the verge of nervous breakdowns or anything, but there was a lot going on up there that we had to sort out individually and as a couple too.

Having done almost all of that before we took our plunge into the adoption world, everything since has been relatively plain sailing – the third reason why I am so happy today. In fact, we have been so lucky and everything has gone so smoothly (so far – touch wood and all that stuff) that we are probably the worst possible advert for adoption there could ever be. You have to be prepared for all kinds of problems – and we were – yet our experience of building a family in this way has been quite amazing and largely trouble-free. Not that we're complacent, and we continue to be alive to our little boy's needs, but we know that sometimes adoption brings with it many greater challenges.

So again, why exactly am I telling you all this? I think it's because I have finally realised – after a long, long time trying to figure this out – that having a child, or building a family, however you choose to do it, is something you have to prepare for in your heart, more so than in any other part of your body. Our son is adopted, but it would make no difference to Mike or me if he had grown from one of our own embryos. He is our son, he is so special and he is the biggest reason why I am so happy today.

Lesley Butcher
April 2010